Leonardo Electronic Almanac

Volume 21 Issue 2

May 15, 2016

ISSN 1071-4391

ISBN 978-1-906897-63-5

Copyright 2016 ISAST

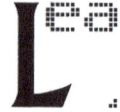 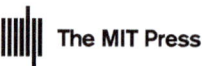

Leonardo Electronic Almanac (LEA) is published by The MIT Press, One Rogers Street, Cambridge, MA 02142-1209, U.S.A., for Leonardo, the International Society for the Arts, Sciences and Technology (Leonardo/ISAST).

LEONARDO®
THE INTERNATIONAL SOCIETY FOR THE
ARTS, SCIENCES AND TECHNOLOGY

Leonardo is a trademark of ISAST registered in the U.S. Patent and Trademark Offices.

For information about Leonardo/ISAST publications and programs, visit www.leonardo.info or email isast@leonardo.info.

With generous support from _____

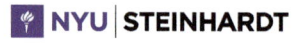 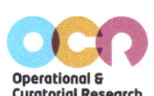 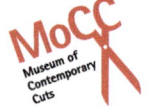 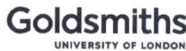

LEA PUBLISHING INFORMATION

Editor in Chief
Lanfranco Aceti lanfranco.aceti@leoalmanac.org

Co-Editor
Özden Şahin ozden.sahin@leoalmanac.org

Managing Editor
John Francescutti john.francescutti@leoalmanac.org

Editorial Manager
Çağlar Çetin caglar.cetin@leoalmanac.org

Art Director
Deniz Cem Önduygu deniz.onduygu@leoalmanac.org

Editorial Board
Peter J. Bentley, Ezequiel Di Paolo, Ernest Edmonds, Felice Frankel, Gabriella Giannachi, Gary Hall, Craig Harris, Sibel Irzık, Marina Jirotka, Beau Lotto, Roger Malina, Terrence Masson, Jon McCormack, Mark Nash, Sally Jane Norman, Christiane Paul, Simon Penny, Jane Prophet, Jeffrey Shaw, William Uricchio

Graphic Designer & Cover Design
Siyi Wang

Production
Passero Productions

Executive Editor
Roger Malina roger.malina@leoalmanac.org

Editorial Office
Leonardo Electronic Almanac
Boston University, Arts Administration
808 Commonwealth Avenue, Room 269E, Boston, MA 02215
www.bu.edu/artsadmin
P 617-353-4064 F 617-358-1230 E aceti@bu.edu

Email
info@leoalmanac.org

Web
www.leoalmanac.org
www.twitter.com/LEA_twitts
www.flickr.com/photos/lea_gallery
www.facebook.com/pages/
  Leonardo-Electronic-Almanac/209156896252

LEONARDO ELECTRONIC ALMANAC, VOLUME 21 ISSUE 2

Mary Sherman: What if You Could Hear a Painting

EDITED BY LANFRANCO ACETI

To Tamar Tembeck and Siyi Wang
without whom this catalogue would not have been possible

and to George Bossarte and the late Peter Lindenmuth
without whom my dreams might never have been realized

Contents

INTRODUCTION

12   **Preface** by Lanfranco Aceti

15   **Dream Mechanics/Mécaniques oniriques** by Tamar Tembeck

LISTENING

18   **THE FUGUE**

28   **DELAY**

32   **In Praise of Frozen Sound** by Mary Sherman with contributions by Florian Grond

48   **Mary Sherman's Delay (in Collaboration with Florian Grond, 2015–2016), or the Audification of the Gaze** by Lorella Abenavoli

52   **THE (UN)GREEN BOX**

DREAMING

58   **ERI, AFTER DARK**

64   **The Demise of a Dream, or Paradise Regained** by Mary Sherman

WAITING

72   **WAITING FOR YVES**

76   **UNTITLED (DRAWING)**

80   **FOR THOMAS**

84   **NOCTURNE**

CONTEXTUALIZING

92   **AT HEART, SPIKE JONES**

96	**What If?** by Mary Sherman
100	**THE COASTER PROJECT**
102	**HOUSE OF CARDS**

MECHANIZING

106	**LE MATIN DE LA NUIT/BALLET MÉCANIQUE**
110	**AN URBAN SKY**
116	**AN URBAN SKY MINIATURE**

TALKING

120	**Interview** by Lanfrano Aceti with Mary Sherman

SHOOTING FOR THE STARS

128	**TAIPEI**
132	**MECHANICAL UNIVERSE, PART I**
136	**STARS**
140	**REMOTE CONTROLLED SHOOTING STARS**
144	**LIGHT SHADE MODULATOR**
148	Sound, Images and Data: All Dressed up and Ready to Go (A Cautionary Tale) by Mary Sherman
152	**CALLER ID**
160	APPENDIX

INTRODUCTION

Preface

Mary Sherman's work straddles painting, sculpture, installation and performance. Painting, however, remains its driving force – the form's past mysteries, present forms and future possibilities are at the root. Conventional definitions of artistic disciplines are thus overturned along the way. Modular in nature and formal in configuration, her work makes painting's latent touch audible through sound. With the aid of mechanics and digital tools, it is brought into the 21st century, into the realm of time and space – but never at the expense of its physical or psychological charge. The work is meant – like the face of a beloved – to stimulate our curiosity, make us smile, give us reason to pause. To even, perhaps, illuminate a truth.

This book and the accompanying media [1] serve as a catalog for Sherman's show *Dream Mechanics/ Mécaniques oniriques* at OBORO, curated by Tamar Tembeck – and more. Inspired by Florian Dombois' book *What are the Places of Danger... Works 1999–2009*, it is a snapshot of a turning point in Sherman's career, when her paintings started to come off the wall and sound became an integral component of her work. "Though my work may seem to suggest otherwise, I think of myself a painter," she writes. "I am in love with the medium, with the fact that despite repeated cries of its death, painting has endured throughout the centuries, able to respond, adapt and speak across time and place. I am sure that painting continues to have this power to captivate us because it stimulates three senses: most overtly, the visual, more covertly and, perhaps, more indelibly, the aural and tactile. And it is this sensate tease – this suggestion and refusal to be explicit – that forms the core of my work: I am interested in exploiting these relational interactions to make concrete painting's latent 'music'; to make tangible its touch through the audible; to bring painting into the 21st century, into the realm of time with sound."

Increasingly, such ideas have necessitated her learning to machine, program and work with collaborators – such as engineers, composers, sound artists and, in some cases, with artists around the world as part of the large-scale projects for TransCultural Exchange." [2]

This aspect of her work – its existing in multiple locations, being kinetic and incorporating sounds – makes it almost impossible to really grasp the full scope Sherman's work in book form. This, of course, is a problem with nearly all multi-sensory art and (one could argue) with books on art in general. Much of the pleasure of experiencing the work is lost, but new insights can still be gained. To help in this endeavor, this book includes links to the works' audio and video components [3] and and a limited edition DVD. And, perhaps, one could say this is how a tome of her work should be. Sherman's work often addresses the existential reality that true understanding is malleable and beyond any certain grasp, but it is nonetheless compelling.

Lanfranco Aceti
Editor in Chief, Leonardo Electronic Almanac
Director, Museum of Contemporary Cuts

REFERENCES AND NOTES

1. The media is available at http://transculturalexchange.org/marysherman/catalog.html.
2. TransCultural Exchange is an artist-run organization that Sherman founded in Chicago in 1988 to facilitate an exchange exhibit and related programming between Chicago and Vienna. Since then the organization has grown, producing over 200 projects in more than 60 countries and necessitating its incorporation as a 501(c)(3) nonprofit in 2002. Today, it is based in Boston and is perhaps best known as the producer of an *International Conference of Opportunities in the Arts* biennale.
3. http://transculturalexchange.org/marysherman/catalog.html.

Dream Mechanics/ Mécaniques oniriques

by Tamar Tembeck

Dream Mechanics/Mécaniques oniriques, a retrospective exhibition at OBORO in Montreal, presents a selection of works from the past decade by the American artist Mary Sherman. Though solidly grounded in her practice as a painter, Sherman's aesthetic approach offers a sensory and spatial expansion of the traditional territory of painting. By introducing diverse kinetic and auditory elements to the experience of her works, Sherman manages to give flesh to the unsuspected synesthesia of the painterly medium.

Sherman's production has often been described as being at the threshold of 20th and 21st century formal preoccupations. Whereas at the height of 20th century American Modernism, painting was famously thought to exalt the two-dimensional qualities that are proper to it (according to the art critic Clement Greenberg), Sherman's painterly constructions present a polysensorial potential that rather begs a more expansive approach. All the while referring to the history of modern art in her works (notably through her choice of titles, which pay tribute, amongst others, to the Dadaists), Sherman's practice is distinctly contemporary and reliant upon present-day technologies. Her projects generally include abstract paintings characterized by generous impasto but arranged in compositions that are either modular (*The White Paintings*) or mechanical (*Mechanical Universe*; *Nocturne*; *At Heart, Spike Jones*; *Le Matin de la Nuit/Ballet Mécanique*; *Eri, After Dark*). Other works, which she develops in collaboration with audio artists, include prominent sound elements that add melodious layers to the pure *bruitisme* of their mechanical articulations (*Waiting for Yves*; *Mechanical Universe*; *Nocturne*; *Eri, After Dark*). Sherman's recent project *Delay* pushes the exploration of the sensory links between eyes and ears even further by featuring a spatialized sonification of a small painted work.

The integration of sound into Sherman's production offers a new means to translate, and, in a sense, to magnify the inherent tactile and sensory qualities that she perceives in painting. The mechanical animation of her painted objects also gives them a mobile and sculptural presence in space that detaches them from the habitual fixity of a wall hanging. The environments that result from these constructions generate qualities that are at times playful, at times dreamy. Hence the title for this retrospective: *Dream Mechanics/ Mécaniques oniriques* presents a constellation of singular creations that oscillate between the materiality of their incarnation and their intimations of the sublime. The works chosen for the exhibition at OBORO specifically highlight Sherman's expansion of the painterly territory by incorporating both kinetic and audio arts. Ultimately, in Sherman's work, the field in which painting is experienced extends well beyond the eye, awakening the tactile, auditory and kinesthetic senses of its viewers.

LISTENING

The Fugue

Sound (by Benoit Granier), black mirror, wood platform, oil paint, speakers (by Florian Grond), aluminum, microprocessors, sound modules, plastic cases and circuitry

Total dimensions variable; Central element: 7" × 36" × 80"

Video documentation: http://www.transculturalexchange.org/marysherman/works/current/fugue/vd.html

2015–2016

DESCRIPTION

The Fugue consists of a suspended wooden platform with an arrangement of aluminum channel on top and an assortment of circuitry below. Between the spaces created by the staggered aluminum structures, five miniature white paintings [1] are motorized and choreographed (using micro-processors and motors that are triggered by sensors) to appear, disappear, reverse and re-appear, not unlike the musical structure of a fugue. Behind this, in the same dimmed room, is a large black mirror that reflects the setup and the audience watching it. And, accompanying all this – via five speakers (borrowed from and echoing *The Fugue*'s antecedent *Delay*) [2] – is Benoît Granier's *Unmentioned, what it can become as though it were not... (Fugue)*. Granier's musical composition is based on the sounds the sound artist Florian Grond generated from scans of five areas of the white painting that forms the core of the installation *Delay*. [3] In other words, Granier took Grond's sounds and turned them into a fugue. Or, put yet another way, Granier took a painting's typically inaudible voice (made audible for *Delay*) and set it to music, [4] which in turn inspired *The Fugue*.

The Fugue then is a further exploration of painting in the realm of time and space; and, in this case, it is also meant to suggest something fragile, magical and trapped within a skin that, despite all the ways it is presented – like the multi-dimensional, sensory quest to understand painting – remains a mystery. The work also purposely references Plato's cave, art's ability to traverse time and the poignant reality that things and people continuously morph, change, astonish and delight us.

ACKNOWLEDGEMENTS

Florian Grond for the speakers and sonification of *Delay* (which Benoît Granier used as the basis for *The Fugue*) and Siyi Wang for video documentation.

EXHIBITION VENUES

OBORO (as part of *Dream Mechanics/Mécaniques oniriques*), Montreal, Canada, curated by Tamar Tembeck, 2016

AWARDS

Berkshire Taconic Community Foundation Artist's Resource Trust Grant, 2016

Boston College Office of International Programs Summer Research Grant, 2016

REFERENCES AND NOTES

1. The five small paintings in *The Fugue* are made from the same piece *Delay* came from – *The White Painting(s)*. That work consists of long, white, rectangular-shaped paintings that can slide along similarly sized strips of polished aluminum. Pushed all together, the white panels create a large rectangular painting; pushed apart, they become an arrangement of narrow, individual paintings contrasted by the polished aluminum, which also reflects its surroundings.

2. See *Delay*, pp. 28–31.

3. As explained in *In Praise of Frozen Sound*, pp. 32–47.

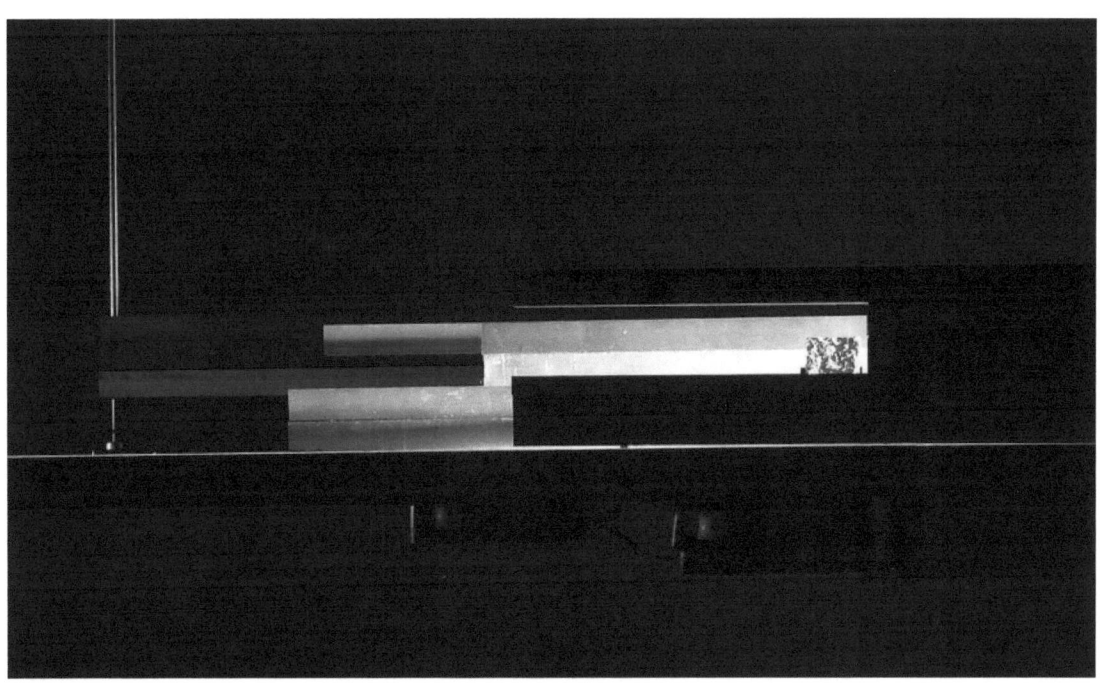

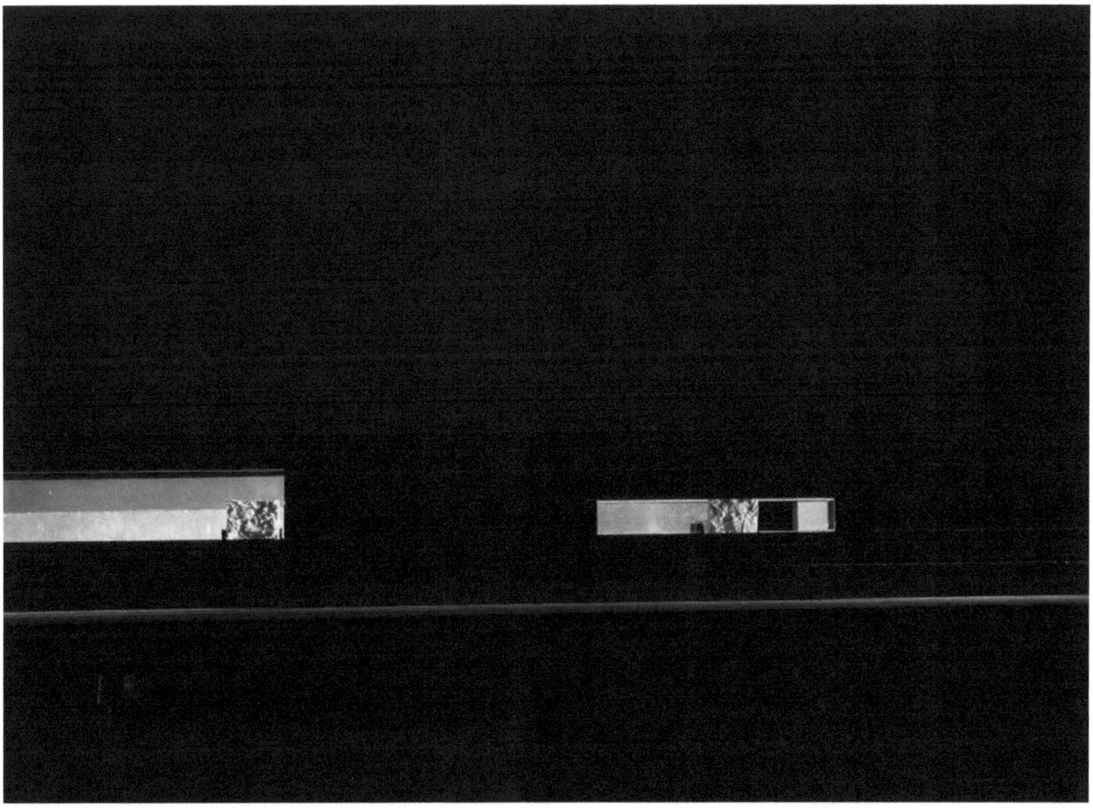

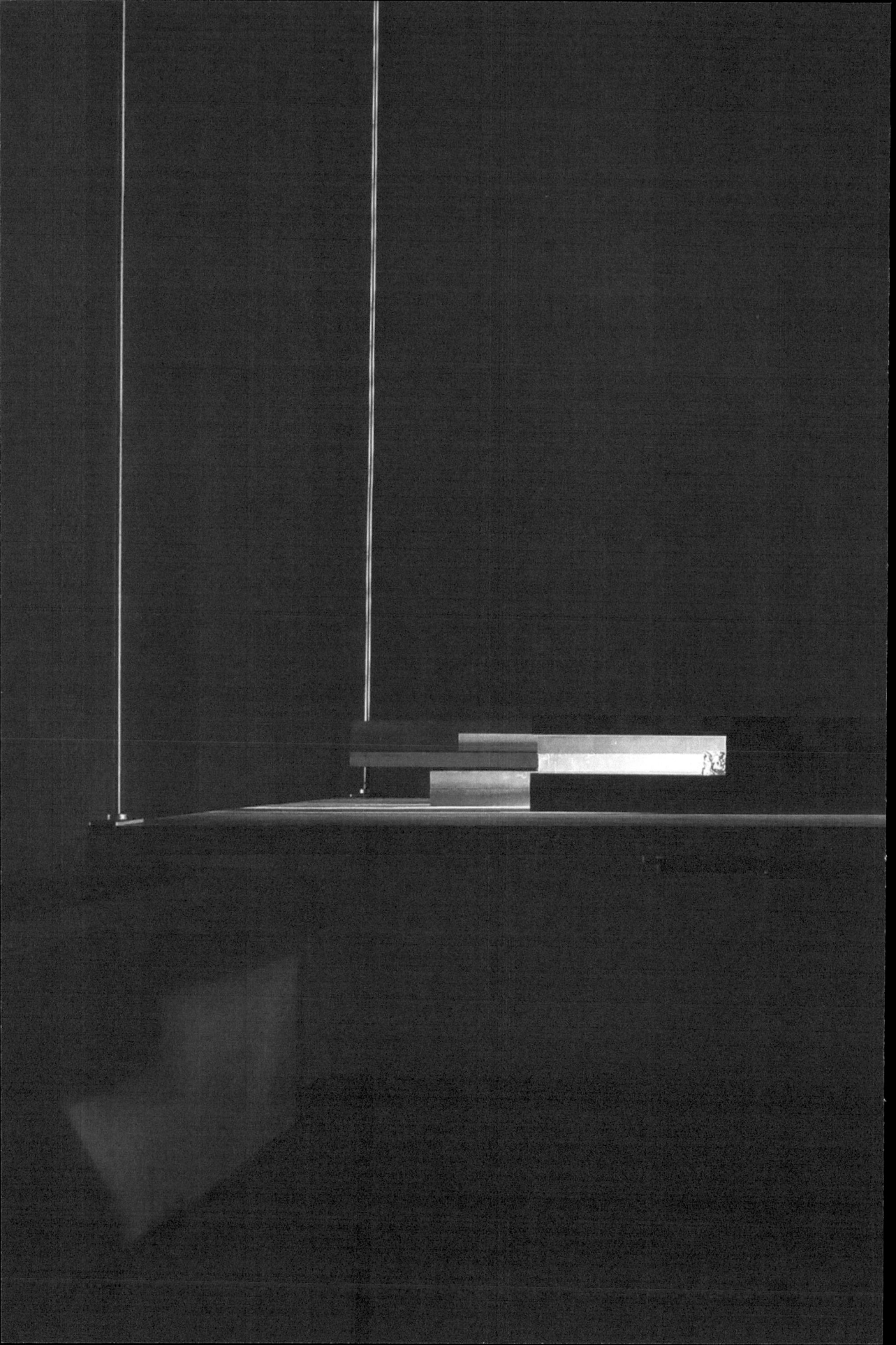

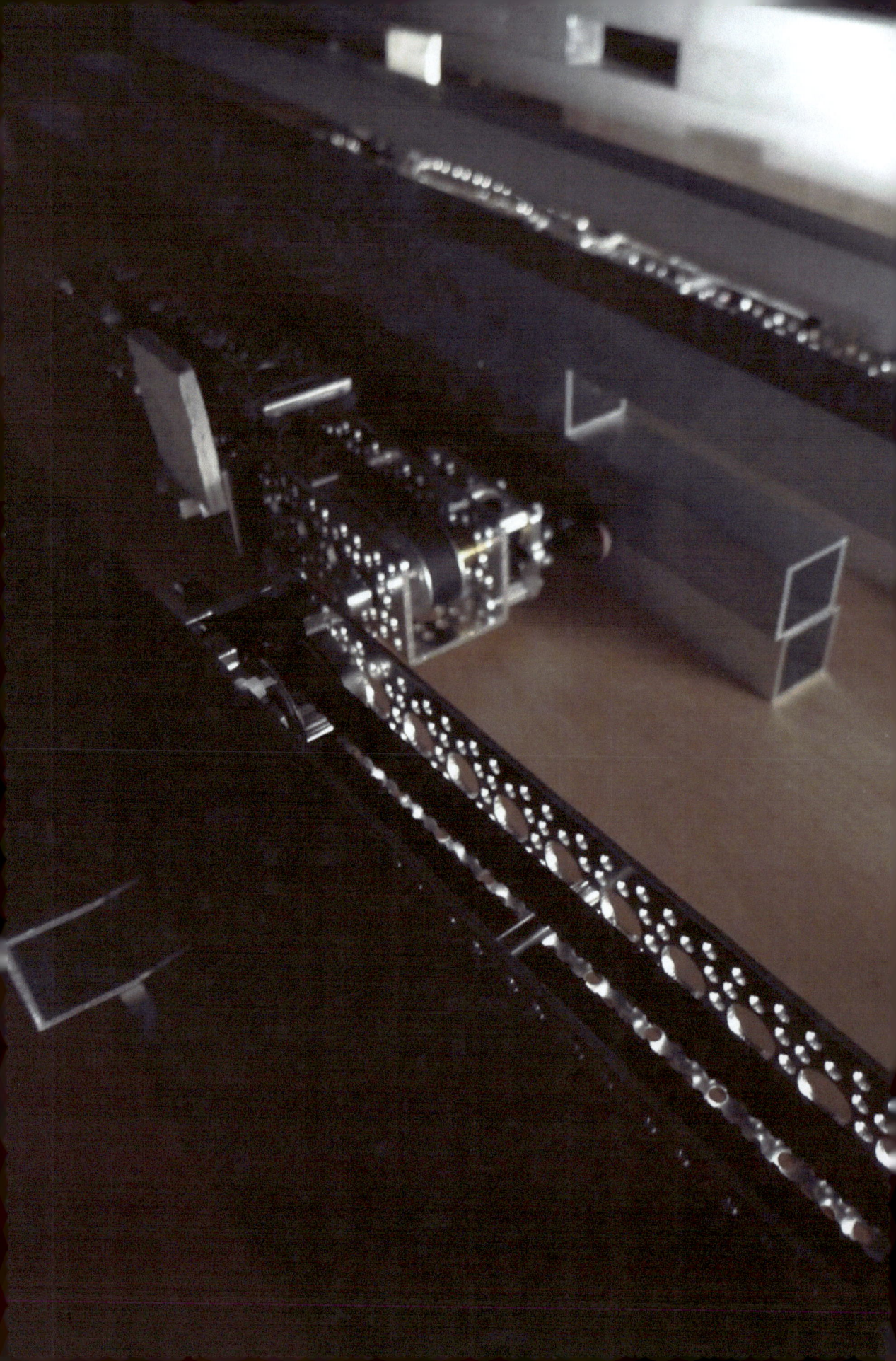

4. About his fugal composition *Unmentioned, what it can become as though it were not.. Fugue* (for electronic and multi-channel diffusion), Granier writes:

> If I'm not real good, I prefer to be just frankly no good. I don't want to disguise myself as a man of learning. I don't want to be the representative of a hobby. I want to be what nature made me—no good.
>
> – Aldous Huxley, Point Counter Point (London: Chatto & Windus, 1952), pp. 91–92.

"Dissociative Amnesia, subtype psychogenic fugue, is characterized by reversible amnesia. This state usually lasts from a few hours to numerous days, although it can also last for months or even longer." [i] Typically, it involves unplanned travel or wandering, and in some cases the person adapts a new identity.

My fugal composition tries to recreate that feeling of wandering, or this form of amnesia's unplanned travel, within the closed structure of a fugue. It also uses the formal organization of Huxley's work in that it creates a kind of musical discussion that evolves over time through a series of exchanges and arguments. Instead of a single line or motive, there are a number of interlinked storylines within a central theme.

Similarly, a fugue is a contrapuntal piece of music that uses melodies, which are then developed episodically using composition techniques such as imitations. Thus, following Huxley's books and ideas, the present composition features six themes (sounds that were chosen on the basis of their different spectral contents, with each sound having a different color). (See figure 1.) These sounds are added together to create a melody that is used throughout the piece as a leitmotif. As seen in the graphic notations created for Mary Sherman's *The Fugue*, their appearance follows classical fugue notation with the exception that each of the six notes is replaced by a specific sound – selected to avoid (as much as possible) any harmonic relationship (see figure 2).

Very important to the composition is the recreation of a feeling of wandering, loss and searching. This is created using a drone (a long note that delimitates musical cells). The drone is central to the piece's form and concept. It is made up of a series of 16 drones – each derived from the six sounds of the leitmotif but of a slightly different timbre (see figure 3).

The drone acts as the basic building block of the composition's structure and represents the passing of time, where sound is continuously similar, distinctive, unique and at the same time different. It is used to punctuate and emphasize the dramatic effects constructed by the work's six sounds, or characters, underscoring important changes within the musical process. It is also meant to suggest a discussion, where the audience can imagine the unfolding of acceptation, refusal, identification, argumentation and finally the conclusion of all six characters slowly and calmly pausing as they undergo stages of denial, isolation, anger and acceptance.

Additionally, harmonic materials (based upon the superposition of four notes) create additional motifs where the timbre is constantly changing, building a relationship between the drone cell and the motivic one. The creation of diverse timbres is achieved through serialized filters (see figure 4).

i. David Spiegel et al., "Dissociative Disorders in DSM-5," *Annual Review of Clinical Psychology* 9 (2013), pp. 299–326.

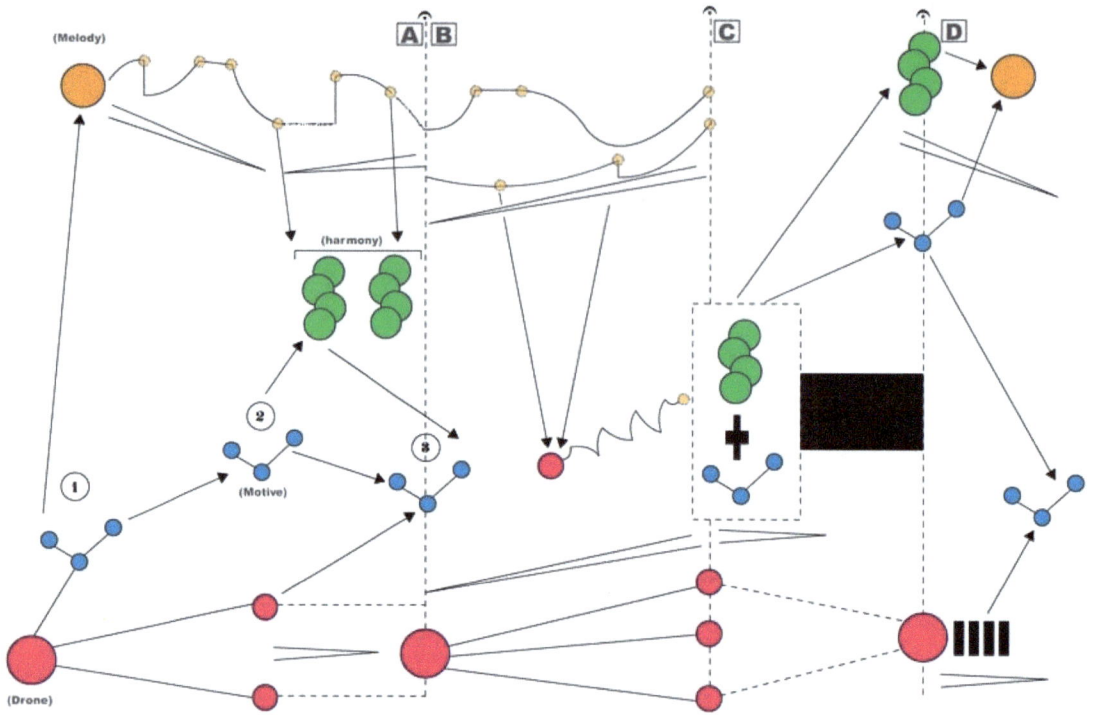

The score for *Unmentioned, what it can become as though it were not.. Fugue* by Benoit Granier, 2016.

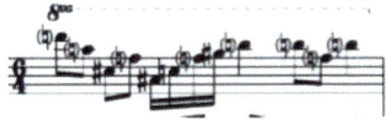 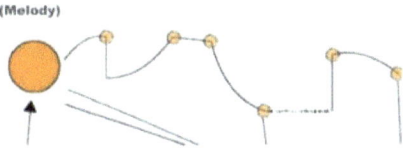

Figure 1 depicts the melodic construction of the original (acoustic) sketch and the electronic version's transposition of it. (As seen, the electronic version keeps the melodic contours, rather than adjusting to the strict pitch relationships of the acoustic version).

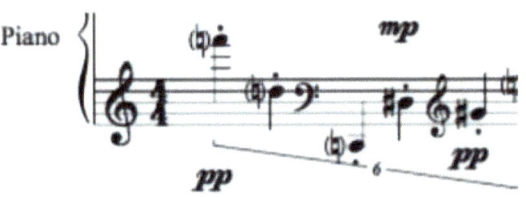 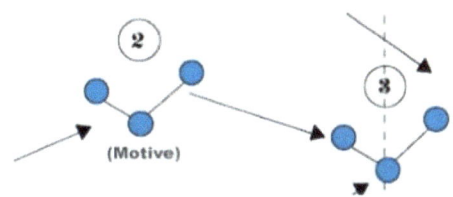

Figure 2 depicts a motif from the original acoustic sketch and its representation in the electronic version. (Again, the motifs retain only the melodic contours in the electronic version and avoid the precise pitch relationships of the original sketch.)

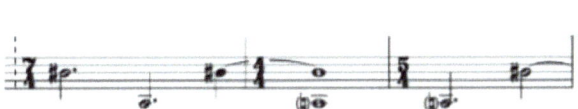 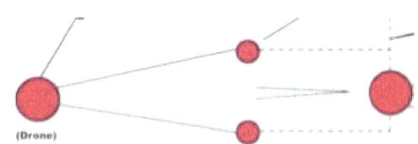

Figure 3 is an example of the drone in the original sketch and its electronic version's transposition.

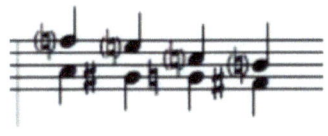 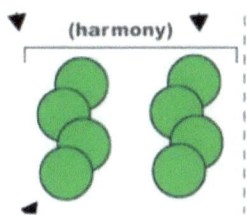

Figure 4 is an example of the harmonic material, built on the four notes' superimposition and variations.

Delay

Sonification and speakers (by Florian Grond), oil paint on wood, spotlight, AC and DC motors, aluminum, microprocessors and circuitry

Total dimensions variable; Central element: 192" (adjustable) × 24" × 24";
5 speakers: 12" × 12" × 3" each

Video documentation: https://vimeo.com/118346045

2012–2014 (2015–2016 remounting/circuitry redesigned to be floor mounted)

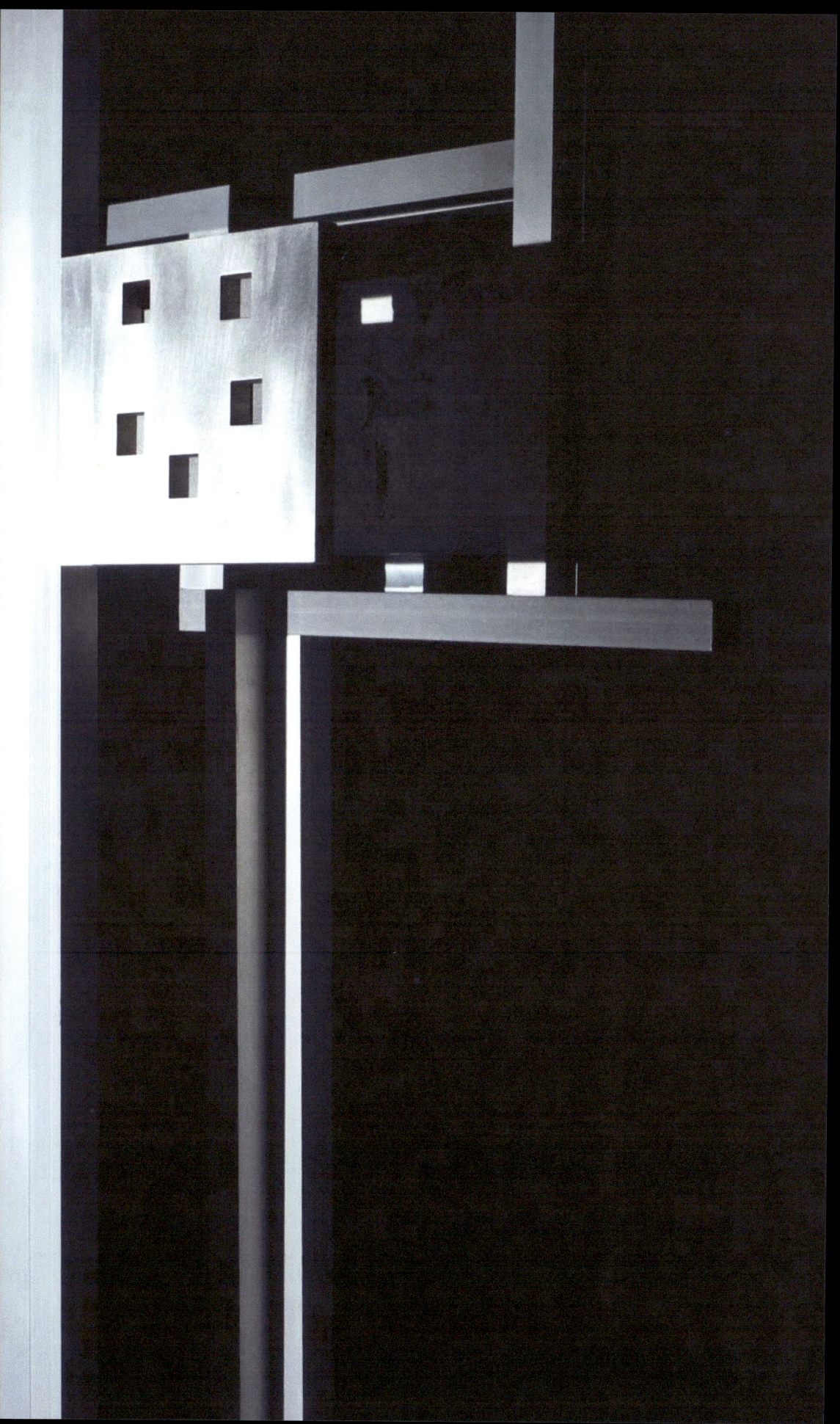

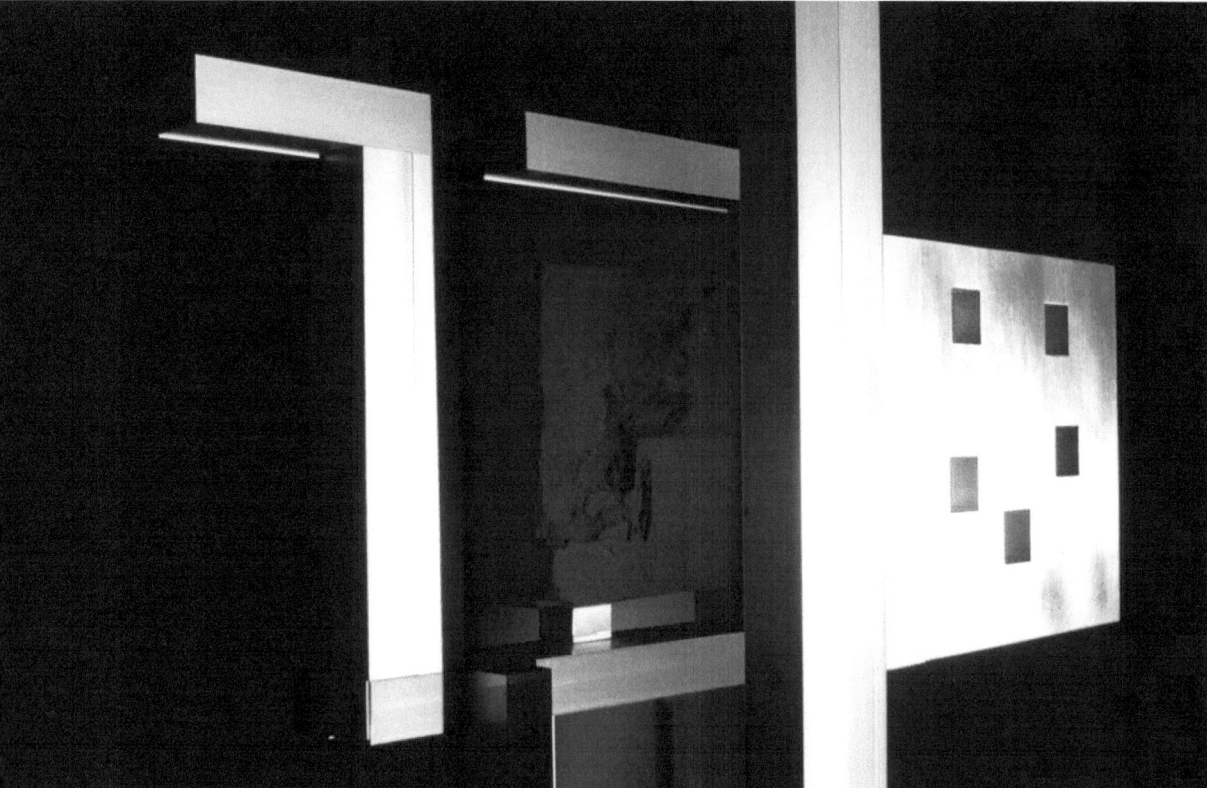

DESCRIPTION

Delay is collaboration with the sound artist and researcher Florian Grond. It consists of a scanned painting, spot lit and suspended in a darkened room. When someone approaches, an aluminum plate with five small shutters swings in front of the painting. As the shutters slowly open and close, creating an eclipse-like effect, they reveal portions of the painting that had previously been scanned. Simultaneously, the sounds generated (sonified) from the scanned data can be heard on five multi-channeled, surround-sound speakers.

Displayed like a precious jewel, *Delay* presents a painting as a cherished artifact. The mechanisms surrounding it create intense areas of focus, augmented by the painting's "voice," which echoes around the walls. A chair is provided to encourage one to linger.

The piece is the result of an all-encompassing obsession with oil paint, which can be likened to any love and its accompanying desire to intimately know everything about the beloved – in this case, even what a painting sounds like. It also references Marcel Duchamp's *The Large Glass, The Bride Stripped Bare by Her Bachelors, Even* (whose original title was also *Delay* and which also dealt with impossible love) and is, of course, more – but never enough.

ACKNOWLEDGEMENTS

Brett Bouma and Martin Villiger at The Wellman Center for Photomedicine (Massachusetts General Hospital Harvard Medical School) for the Fourier-domain Optical Coherence Tomography Scanning; Kathy Patterson and George Bossarte for technical/systems controls assistance and special thanks to Andrew Anselmo, L. Alexis Emelianoff, Marc Fournel, Matthias Kronlachner, Regina Moeller (KiT Gallery Curator), Peter Plessas, Rudi Punzo (website documentation), William Stephens (access to Nexus Machine Shop) and Siyi Wang (video documentation and graphic design). The first exhibition in Trondheim, Norway was kindly supported by a travel grant from the Conseil des arts et des lettres du Québec (CALQ).

EXHIBITION VENUES

OBORO, presented as part of the International Digital Art Biennial (BIAN) and the Montreal Digital Spring, Montreal, Canada, 2016

Galleri KiT, Norwegian University of Science and Technology, Trondheim, Norway, curated by Regina Moeller, 2014

PAPERS

Ripples: What Artists Bring to the Community, The Kansai International Symposium: Cultural Crossroads = A.I.R., Yonago Convention Center, Yonago, Japan, November 28, 2015

Audifying Painting: Hybrid Curatorial Practices for Sound Art, presented at the Histories, Theories and Practices of Sound Art Curating Conference, Goldsmiths, University of London and the Courtauld Institute of Art, May 15–17, 2014

Sound, Images and Data: All Dressed up and Ready to Go (keynote presentation) at the Sound, Images and Data Conference, New York University, New York, July 23–25, 2015

AWARDS/HONORS

Included in Creative Capital's 2013, 2014 and 2015 On Our Radar, a searchable database featuring noteworthy Moving Image and Visual Arts projects.

RELATED WORKSHOPS

Delay, Norwegian University of Science and Technology, Trondheim, Norway, November 2014, http://www.kit.ntnu.no/en/content/delay-workshop-mary-sherman-and-florian-grond

PRESS

Abenavoli, Lorella. "*Delay* (2012) de Mary Sherman ou l'audification du regard." *ETC MEDIA* 108, *Dans les internets / Inside the Internet* (June–September 2016): p. 93.

Beerlink, Anna. "Forschen mit den Ohren." *Neue Zeitschrift für Musik* 5 (November 2015): pp. 65–66.

Sherman, Mary. "In Praise of Frozen Sound." *Leonardo Electronic Almanac* (forthcoming).

In Praise of Frozen Sound: Audifying Painting, Hybrid Curatorial Practices for Sound Art

by Mary Sherman
with contributions by Florian Grond

The study of painting most often focuses on its visual qualities: the things that one can see, its subject matter and form or compositional elements. From there, analysis typically extends to the context in which the work was made, the era in which it was created, the technical advances of the time, the biographical quirks of its creator, etc.

I propose, however, that something more fundamental is being overlooked – that the enduring charm of a Cézanne painting of apples, for instance, is not due to its representation of a familiar subject. Nor is it because of its pioneering depiction of space and the aftermath of that breakthrough. Instead it continues to attract its viewers due to its tactile, physical structure, its embodiment of process, its transcendent orchestration of surface incidents: some short, some long, some smooth, some rough, some delicate, some brutal, but all exquisitely composed, scored and re-lived with each viewing.

This frozen record of the act of painting – which, in the best of instances, is a masterful one – is what I believe makes painting so compelling. Beyond the dazzling ordering of colors and shapes, the enjoyment of visually surfing along a painting's structural incidents, while at the same time that one cannot touch them, instantaneously creates desire. And that desire doesn't stop there. It is compounded by a similar tickling of the ear, the sense that complements the eye in our experience of time and space. [1] In this way, I argue that painting stimulates three senses: most overtly, the visual; more covertly and perhaps more indelibly, the aural and tactile. And it is this tease – this suggestion and refusal to be explicit – that allows the viewer's mind the pleasure of possible closure, while that possibility always slips beyond one's certain grasp… like any love.

Of course, many disciplines have studied how the senses complement, augment, and interact with each other. [2] Together – as sound in film so brilliantly exploits – they can be more efficient than alone, which neuropsychologists Mattieu DuBois, David Poeppel and Denis Pelli also note. [3] However, for my work, what is perhaps most thrilling is how the interactions between the senses can seem to resemble those between people; like some of our interactions, they can at times complement each other, and at other times deceive each other when integrating conflicting input. [4] Or, as Michel Chion notes, "We never see the same thing when we also hear; we don't hear the same thing when we see as well." [5] However, in many cases the senses are in mutual exchange, which Chion goes on to define as "trans-sensory perceptions." [6]

It is this multi-faceted and poignant exchange between the senses that fuels me and my collaborator of *Delay*, the sound artist and researcher Florian Grond, to exploit their relational interactions; to make concrete painting's latent "music"; to make tangible its touch through the audible; to bring painting into the 21st century, into the realm of time with sound.

When considered from a curatorial standpoint, sound can then be both an art form in its own right as well as a crucial component for accessing the visual and tactile senses; for opening up fruitful fields of associations and allusions between the various media; and for uncovering alternate ways of making, approaching and perceiving art works. All this, in turn, can provide new entrées for engaging not only with artworks, but also with the world – ways that incorporate sound, sight and touch, none more privileged than another.

A CASE STUDY: FROM CASUAL, SEMIOTIC, AND EMOTIONAL TO AESTHETIC EXPLORATION

Despite repeated cries of its death, painting endures. It is one of civilization's most resilient media, continuing to evolve and fascinate, informed and responding to the advances of its age. From pigment mixed with wax for Egyptian funerary figures to the use of tempera in medieval manuscripts, from the introduction of oil paint in the Renaissance to acrylic's invention in the '60s, painting has adapted to its age's technological advances as readily as it has to its tastes, styles and mores.

The previous generation witnessed painting moving into three dimensions (with works, for example, by Frank Stella, Elizabeth Murray, Jessica Stockholder and Anish Kapoor). Today painting finds itself as readily an element in an installation or – in its perennial role – as a representation of the people and preoccupations of its time (such as in the works of Tracey Emin and Gerhard Richter). What Grond and I are proposing, though, is something different: using sound to explore new ways of unleashing painting's ability to offer essential points of reflection and respite.

Initially academically trained as a painter, my fascination with painting focused on its physicality – how paint can be built up, scored; even cut, nailed and glued. This interest led me to take paint out of its historically and continually resurgent illusionary role into a re-investigation of its object-hood. First, I was playing with it as one of many modular elements that could be arranged and re-arranged. Later, the paintings were perched on pedestals, stretched between walls (see figure 1), motorized and paired with such industrial materials as polished aluminum for contrast and pause. (For instance, in *An Urban Sky*, paintings were hung like horizontal panels from the ceiling and mechanized to flip over to signify the passing of day to night to create an updated version of a baroque ceiling painting. Stepping on a large red button also triggered the sound of rain and thunder.)

Next came similarly-surfaced, box-like paintings (inspired by such musical pieces as George Antheil's *Ballet mécanique*) that were motorized to move sequentially, like parts of a choreographed score (also intended to expand the traditional concept of painting beyond that of a flat, silent, immutable object on a wall). These were followed by three-dimensional paintings embedded with microprocessors and amplifiers that were motorized to move across rooms. For instance, *Nocturne* [7] – a nod to James McNeill Whistler's similarly-titled twilight paintings and my own equal interest in painting and sound – consists of four painted modules whose top thin layer of paint doubles as a speaker membrane.

Each module is also programmed to create a mechanical ballet, or dual *pas de deux*, in which the box-like paintings' polished aluminum sides reflect each other in passing but never meet, matching the melancholy sense of longing suggested by the sounds (contributed by the Belgian composer Yannick Franck). Also, through the use of movement and sound, the paintings encourage audiences to linger with their surface treatments, colors and embodied content.

Another variant is *Waiting for Yves*. A play on Yves Klein's *La spécialisation de la sensibilité à l'état matière première en sensibilité picturale stabilisée, Le Vide* (*The Specialization of Sensibility in the Raw Material State into Stabilized Pictorial Sensibility, The Void*), the work is a surround sound environment in which – like in Samuel Beckett's famous play – the situation is pregnant with possibility, vast nothingness and the realization that one must just go on. In large part *Waiting for Yves* [8] consists of a room lined with

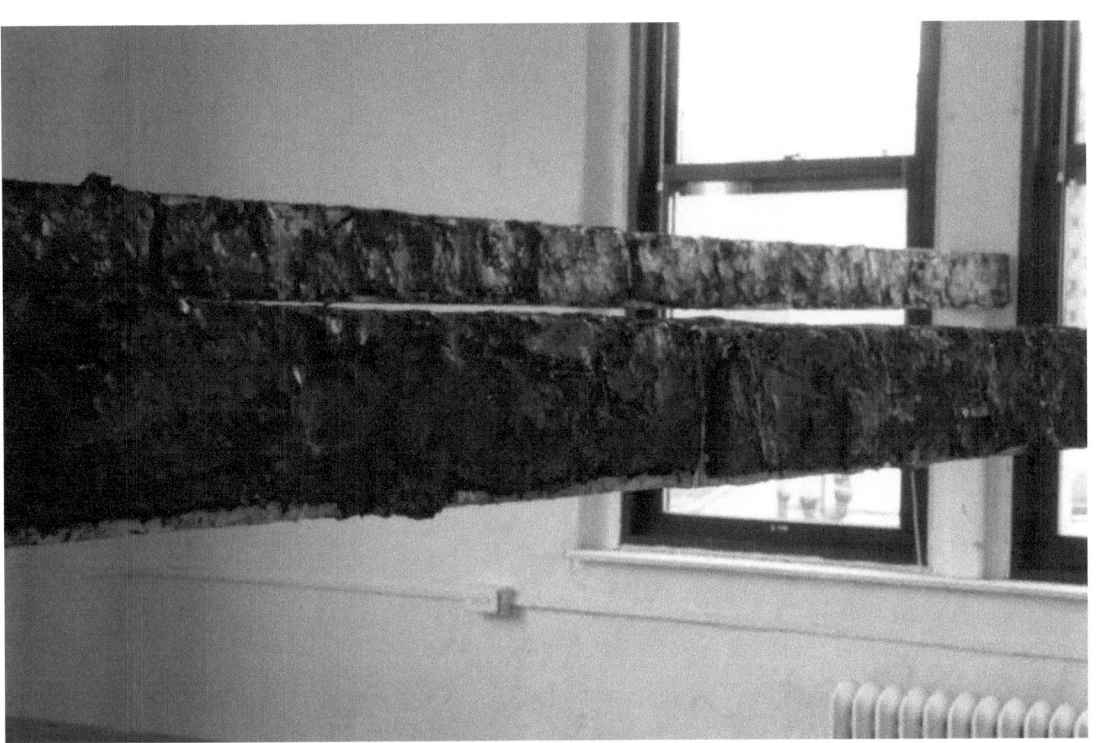

Figure 1 depicts one view of *Bolts of Blue*. The piece consists of two 18-foot-long rectangular wooden boxes (or four-sided paintings). They span the exhibition space, held in place by their own outward pressure against the walls. Three sides are painted with thick chunks of paint. The other side (not shown) is painted with bright blue enamel. Each "bolt" also has a slit in part of it, so that viewers can frame the space in the same way that painters often compose their pictures.

IN PRAISE OF FROZEN SOUND: AUDIFYING PAINTING, HYBRID CURATORIAL PRACTICES FOR SOUND ART

paper that has been covered with hundreds and hundreds of marks of blue oil bar – oil paint in stick form. The room has thus been touched thousands of times. A soundtrack (again by Franck and accessed through headphones) of a walk through snow, punctuated by a couple's inaudible words and a distant train, complete the work, alerting and triggering a number of senses to be more fully engaged.

Thus, the sounds created by my works have a number of characteristics: they are casual (caused by the sound of a motor running, for instance), semiotic (signifying an event of change like the sound of thunder in *An Urban Sky* or the buzzer, motor sound and music box in *Le Matin de la Nuit/Ballet Mécanique*) and, often, emotional (with the sounds matching and augmenting the work's psychological and emotional content). In all these cases, sound offers new points of entry into the paintings' structural and haptic qualities. Further, as in the case of another work, *Eri, After Dark* [9] – which was part of a concert line up at the Beijing Conservatory – the works' appearances in venues traditionally accorded to sound provide new avenues for people to access painting.

In all these works, what also became immediately apparent is that the combination of sound, visual and haptic elements heighten the viewers' engagement, help direct a desired emotional intent and – perhaps not surprisingly, given sound's more affective appeal – lengthen the time the audience spends with the work.

FIRST STEP: AUDIFYING A PAINTING: DELAY

Working in collaboration with Grond, my latest piece, *Delay*, uses sound in the aforementioned ways and more. Here sound is also used as a direct exploration of the structural similarities between the auditory, visual and tactile senses. *Delay* asks: what if you could hear a painting? What if, for instance, you could hear the fragment of this painting (see figures 2 and 3)? [10]

Such scanning of surface structures and topographic data along trajectories to be turned into sound is not new. This idea can be traced back to the writer Rainer Maria Rilke: he speculated about the sound of the sutures on the human skull, which reminded him of the grooves in gramophone records. [11] Later, in the early '90s, Scot Gresham-Lancaster extensively explored the digital terrain of x/y/z values and how they can be turned into sound. [12] Paul DeMarinis transcribed the indentations on the surface of ancient pottery into sound for his work *The Edison Effect*; more recently, Jens Brand has translated the earth's topographic data along the paths of satellites into sounds [13] and Florian Dombois has created a body of artwork based on his application of audification to make audible earthquakes' waveforms. [14]

Likewise, to take advantage of the capacities of the auditory sense to bring about a deeper understanding of visual works, five one-inch sections of one of my paintings (see figure 4) were scanned by the scientist Brett Bouma's assistant Martin Villiger, using Fourier-domain optical coherence tomography, a rich imaging technique. [15]

Figure 2 is a magnified detail of one of the five sections of the painting in *Delay* that was scanned using Fourier-domain optical coherence tomography.

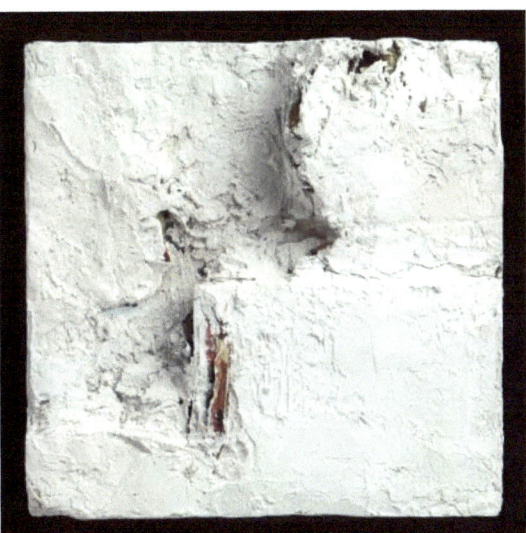

Figure 3 shows the painting that was used as the basis for this first investigation into the sonification of painting.

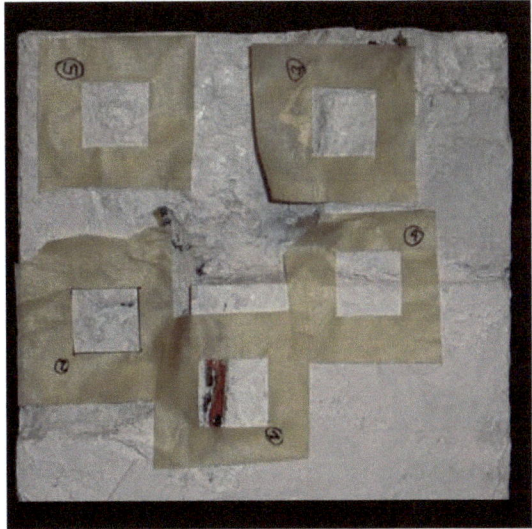

Figure 4 shows the five areas of the same painting shown in Figure 3, with the five areas that were scanned using Fourier-domain optical coherence tomography masked off.

IN PRAISE OF FROZEN SOUND: AUDIFYING PAINTING, HYBRID CURATORIAL PRACTICES FOR SOUND ART

This resulted in five sets of numerical data and corresponding black and white contour images of the same information (see figures 5 and 6), as, for instance, seen below:

---

date: 2010-06-07 00:00:00
sample rate: 50000
latitude: -10 10
longitude: 5
title time channel 1 channel 2 1024

643	696	696	696	610	609	626	626	626	637	637	639
624	639	611	718	718	718	702	638	638	610	610	644
646	646	644	627	619	619	609	609	610	610	610	603
605	609	609	608	436	436	436	606	606	606	608	608
608	436	436	435	434	434	434	434	434	434	433	433
433	434	434	433	432	432	431	432	432	432	432	432
431	430	430	430	430	430	430	430	430	430	430	430
429	429	429	429	429	428	428	428	428	428	429	429
428	428	428	430	430	430	430	431	432	433	433	435
435	435	435	435	435	436	437	438	438	438	438	438
438	438	439	439	438	438	439	439	439	439	439	439
440	440	439	439	439	439	439	439	439	439	439	...

As opposed to ascribing a sound to each number, starting at the upper right corner and proceeding line-by-line through the rows of numbers, Grond instead extracted surface profiles from the data, following predefined paths that are reminiscent of both drawing and the way the eye scans a painting (see figure 7).

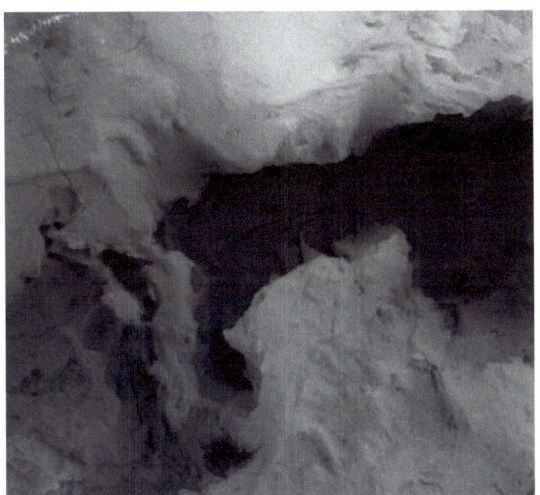

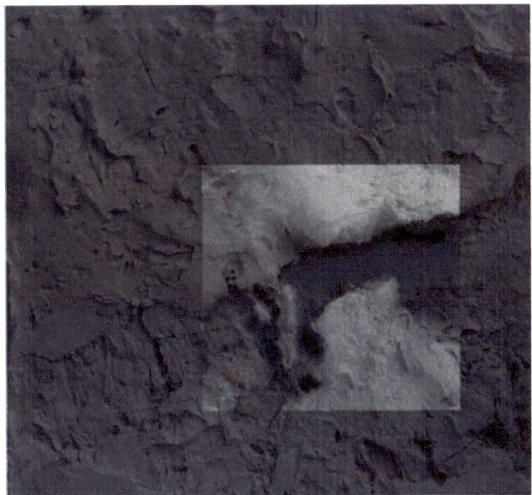

Figure 5 shows the visual mapping of the scientific data derived from the masked square, labeled number 1 in figure 4.

Figure 6 shows the visual mapping of the scientific data derived from the masked square, labeled number 1 in figure 4, which is laid over the actual area of the painting from which the data was derived.

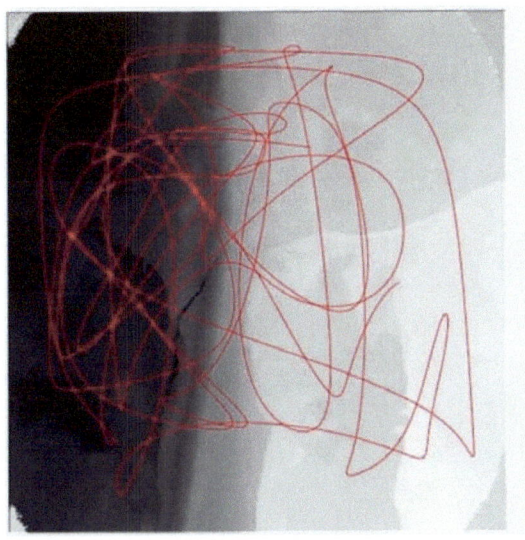

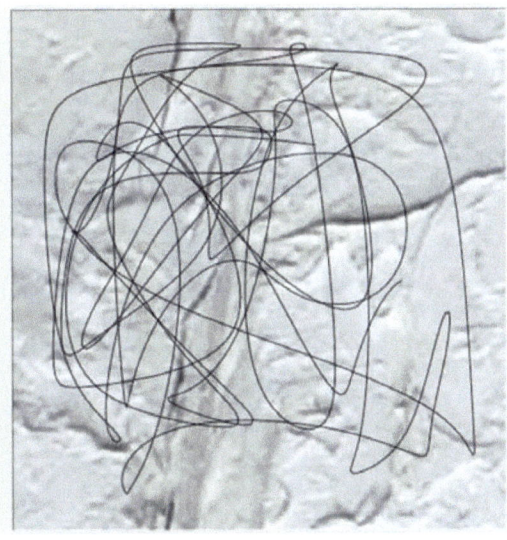

Figure 7 shows the trajectory of the path through the scientific data Grond used as the basis for sonification of the masked square, labeled number 4 in figure 4.

The first graph (see figure 8) shows the contour of the painting's surface – its hills and valleys. The second graph is derived from the first and shows the rate of change on the painting's surface regardless of whether the change is in a so-called hill or valley. The third graph represents how sharp the edges of this change are on the painting's surface and provides the signal from which the audification is made. Thus, for each point that corresponds to a structural event on the painting (caused by the way it was painted, scored and relieved and, also, indicated in the data), a click with a distinct sonic timbre was created.

Grond then took the clicks derived from the painting and manipulated them further. To give a sense of whether the click "resides" in the hills or valleys of the paint surface, reverb was added; the reverberant clicks would now be rather dry in the areas closer to the viewer (the hills) or wet and resonant when further away (in the valleys). Next, to connect these sounds of the surface structure to the colors in the painting (mostly white), the painting's RGB/color frequencies were mapped to spectral envelopes that would be close to human vowel-like sounds. This made the initial clicks a bit less harsh and less immediately bound to an identifiable sonic source. Finally, to make the sounds even less source-binding, they were stretched out a bit more (through granular re-synthesis), which made them even more curious and suited to so many aspects of *Delay*, the title and content of the piece inspired by this research.

The sounds then are not directly identifiable as something concrete. Nonetheless, in their creation, they allude to the idea of the painting's "voice." Or to directly quote Grond, "The irregular occurrence of surface incidents now became repeated articulations of various forms and lengths – all of them at the brink of speaking out, without saying something, but asking for further exploration of the perceived."

As previously mentioned, there is a long history of artists working with extra-sonorous data as a source and inspiration for their compositions and performances. As noted in the *Oxford Handbook of Sound Studies*:

> The practice of using data as raw material for art has a pedigree that reaches back at least as far as the conceptual movements in the 1960s. Sound artists, including John Cage, Alvin Lucier, and Charles Dodge, along with installation artists like Hans Haacke, Sol LeWitt, and Dan Graham, broke away from the prior conception of artists as individuals that realize works according to their own uniquely personal vision. One of Cage's many contributions to the dismantling of the romantic notion of the artist as inspired genius was the work *Atlas Eclipticalis*, in which he superimposed music paper on top of star charts and plotted musical compositions as if they were constellations. In *I Am Sitting in a Room* Alvin Lucier sonified the acoustic characteristics of a room by recording his speech and then playing the recording back into the room, rerecording, playing it back, rerecording, and so on until his vocal signature was thoroughly eroded by successive generations of mediation.
>
> Works like these brought natural and artificial systems to the fore by putting a process or phenomenon ahead of the artists' ostensibly personal 'vision.' What these works also implicitly proposed was that phenomena beyond the perception of the human senses might somehow be represented or reified. [16]

With *Delay*, our aim was to translate the scientific data of the painting in a way that both revealed a relationship between the structure of the painting and the resulting sound, so that experiencing them together would augment and complement (in

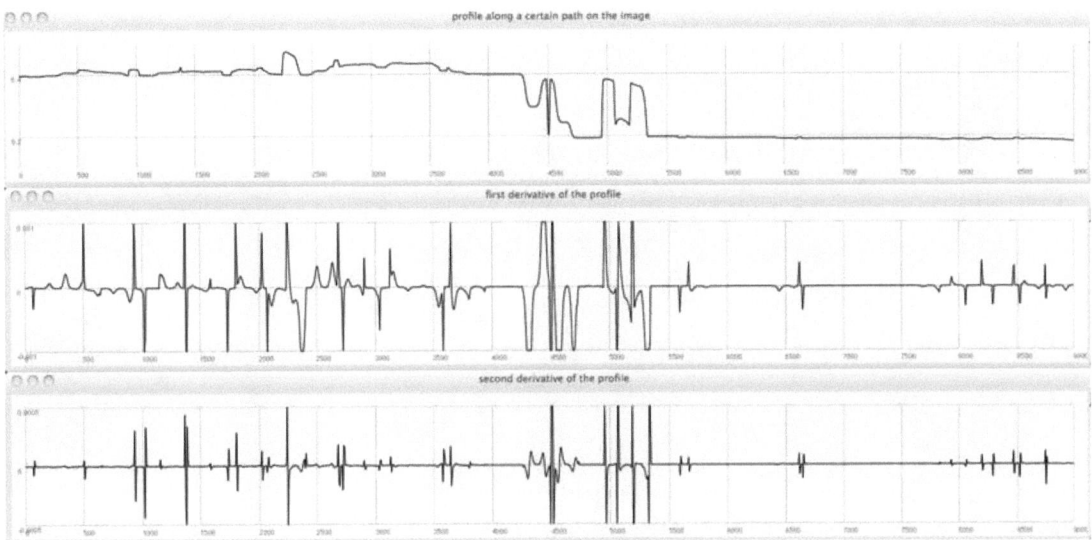

Figure 8 shows the contours of the scanned painting along the trajectories of figure 7 and its derivatives of the scanned painting as described in the text.

the broadest sense of the word) the experience of both. (Thus, closer to the aims of *Delay*, then, would be Ed Ruscha's *Chocolate Room* from the 1970 Venice Biennale and Peter Hopkins' *Perfume Paintings* from the '80s and '90s, as these artists were after something similar, working with painting and olfaction.) [17] In *Delay*, the sound and visuals in this case are meant to be inexorably linked to the audience's experience of the work. On their own, they may have their merits, but their sum is significantly enhanced by the coming together of the parts. This is supported by personal observation of viewings of my own works: the connections between sound and visuals are crucial to the works' success in engaging audiences.

In *Delay* [18] there was also a conscious attempt made to play with the notion of a "tease" – and in this case specifically, which is the paper's argument – that a painting "teases" our aural and tactile senses. Thus, when one enters the installation (figure 9), the painting is presented as an artifact, spot lit and suspended in the middle of a darkened room. When someone enters, a motorized aluminum plate with five small shutters swings in front of the painting, causing the shutters to slowly open and close, one after another, revealing the areas that were scanned, like reverse eclipses (see figures 10 and 11). At the same time, the sounds directly created from the corresponding scans are played on five speakers, which are placed around the room. (These are built as white boxes to visually disappear – e.g. to appear

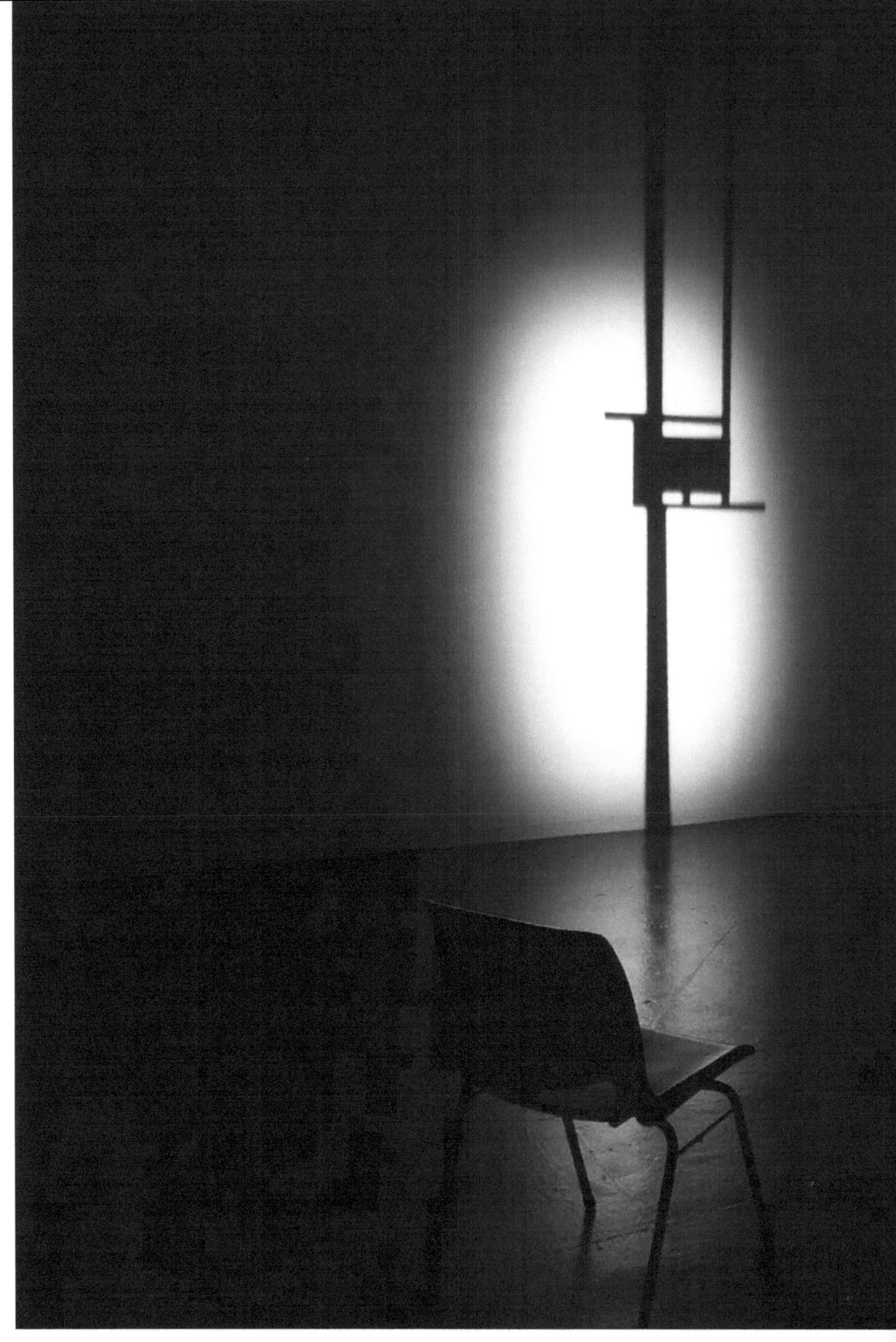

Figure 9 is an installation shot of *Delay*.

to be structural elements of the room's architecture.) The staging of speakers and the spatial orchestration of the sonic movements invite the audience to recompose the painting's surface texture through the sense of listening.

A final, third component consists of a boxed set of all the scale models, drawings, scientific scans, notes, etc. This box provides the materials that relate to the piece's process of production and acts as a bit of a homage to Marcel Duchamp's *Green Box*, which consists of his notes for *The Large Glass*. All aspects of the piece's making then are presented as a metaphor for the attempt to understand the essence of painting. And, like all things and people dear to us, even with so much sensory information – even with the addition of this new scientific data – poignant gaps are bound to remain, which we hope will propel further investigation.

And so as the project started, so it ends: the piece is about love, the overwhelming desire to know something (or someone), the impossibility of doing so, and the nevertheless all-too-human quest to try. Hearing a painting does not take away from its mystery: it simply provides another point of entry, fascination and association. *Delay*, then, is meant to be a lure: to be seen, heard and experienced; to delay people, as love does. What also makes the name *Delay* so apt for this first piece is that Duchamp's *The Bride Stripped Bare by her Bachelors, Even* (*The Large Glass*) was originally entitled *Retard en verre* or *Delay in Glass*; [19] and Duchamp was not only interested in the connection between sound and visuals, but *The Large Glass* likewise dealt with impossible love, which has hovered at the edges of my mind ever since I first conceived this project.

ACKNOWLEDGEMENTS

Brett Bouma and Martin Villiger at The Wellman Center for Photomedicine for the Fourier-domain Optical Coherence Tomography Scanning; Andrew Anselmo, Kathy Patterson and George Bossarte/gb engineering for technical/systems controls and Carlee Ryfa Lobdell and John Shakespear for copyediting.

REFERENCES AND NOTES

1. The complementary potential of the sense of hearing to reveal structures in digital data has also received attention from the field of auditory display, where techniques such as sonification and audification have been developed and refined over the last 20 years. For reference textbooks see: Gregory Kramer, ed., *Auditory Display: Sonification, Edification, and Auditory Interfaces* (Boulder: Westview Press, 1994); and Thomas Hermann, Andy Hunt, and John G. Neuhoff, eds., *The Sonification Handbook* (Berlin: Logos Publishing House, 2011).

2. For an overview that integrates perceptual and phenomenological perspectives on the interplay between sound and sight see: Gregory Daurer, "Audiovisual Perception," in *Audiovisuology Compendium: See This Sound – An Interdisciplinary Survey of Audiovisual Culture*, vol. 1, ed. Dieter Daniels and Sandra Naumann (Cologne: Walther König, 2010), pp. 247–257; Michel Chion, *Film, a Sound Art*, translated by Claudia Gorbman (New York: Columbia University Press, 2009); as well as Hans Beller, "Between the Poles of Mickey Mousing and Counterpoint," in *Audiovisuology 2 Essays*, ed. Dieter Daniels and Sandra Naumann (Cologne: Walther König, 2011), pp. 102–119.

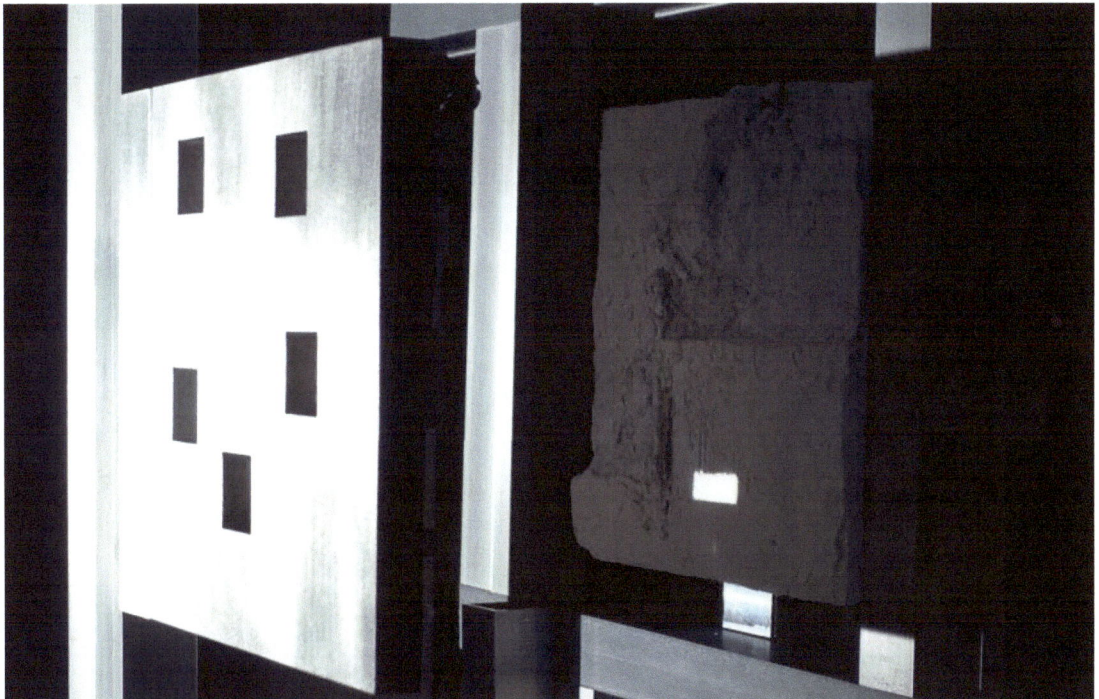

Figure 10 depicts the light shinning through one of the shutters, slowly revealing one of the one-inch square patches of painting that were scanned, generating one of the sets of sounds heard on the speakers arranged throughout the space.

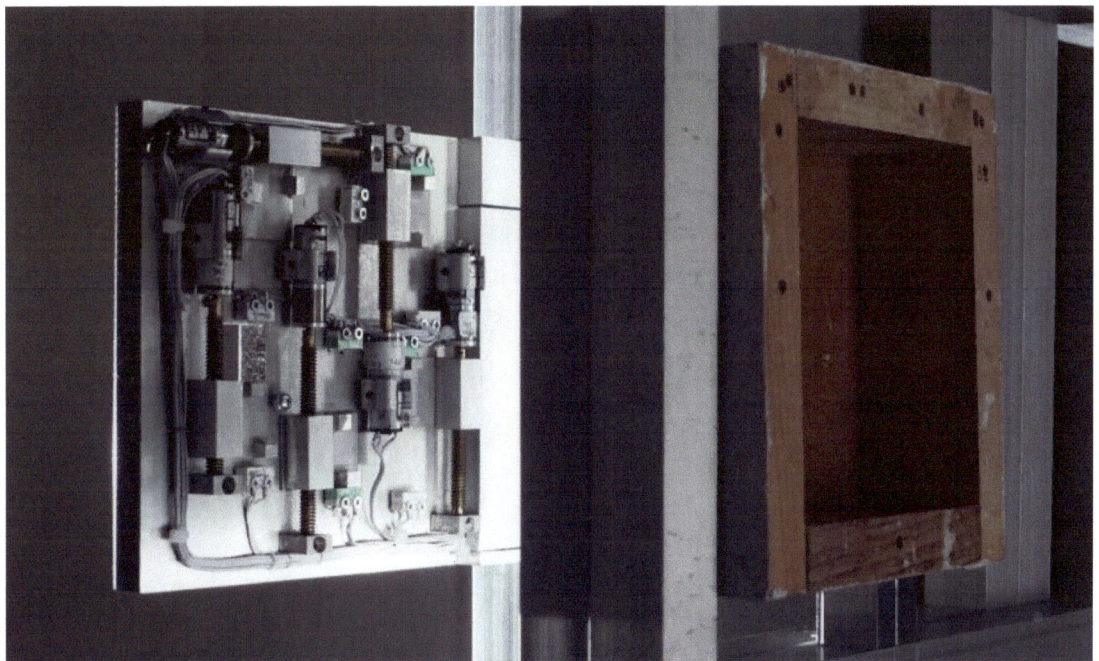

Figure 11 shows the backside of *Delay* (right) and the mechanisms that open and close the five small "shutters" on the aluminum plate in front of the painting at the beginning of each shutter's opening (left).

3. Mattieu DuBois, David Poeppel, and Denis G. Pelli, "Seeing and Hearing a Word: Combining Eye and Ear Is More Efficient than Combining the Parts of a Word," *PLoS ONE* 8, no. 5 (2013). Accessed August 8, 2016, doi: 10.1371/journal.pone.0064803.

4. Harry McGurk and John MacDonald, "Hearing Lips and Seeing Voices," *Nature* 264 (1976): pp. 746-748.

5. Michel Chion, *Audio Vision: Sound on Screen*, trans. Claudia Gorbman (New York: Columbia University Press, 1994).

6. Trans-sensory perceptions, as coined by Chion, are "perceptions that belong to no one particular sense but that may travel via one sensory channel or another without their content or their effect being limited to this one sense… Everything involving rhythm may serve as an example. But other cases involve spatial perceptions as well as the verbal dimension. A word that is read or spoken belongs to the same sphere of language, even if the modes of its transmission (handwriting, vocal timbre) run in parallel sensory channels. Rhythm is the essential trans-sensory dimension, since we experience it before we are born. The fetus encounters rhythm in the form of variations in pressure on the body wall, parsed with the combined beats of the mother's heart and its own… Texture and grain are another category of trans-sensory perception." Michel Chion, *Film, a Sound Art*, p. 496.

7. https://vimeo.com/100345437.

8. https://vimeo.com/111466726.

9. https://vimeo.com/111465489.
   It would sound like this sound file:
   https:// transculturalexchange.org/marysherman/catalog/Delay/Sound.html.

10. Rainer Maria Rilke, "Ur-Geräusch," *Soglio, am Tage Mariae Himmelfahrt* (Switzerland: 1919).

11. Bill Thibault and Scot Gresham-Lancaster "Experiences in Digital Terrain: Using Digital Elevation Models for Music and Interactive Multimedia," *Leonardo Music Journal* 7 (1997): 11–17.

12. Paul DeMarinis and Jens Brand, *BOOK* (Heidelberg: Kehrer Verlag, 2009).

13. Florian Dombois, "Auditory Seismology on Free Oscillations, Focal Mechanisms, Explosions and Synthetic Seismograms," in *Proceedings of the 8th International Conference on Auditory Display: ICAD2002*, ed. R. Nakatsu and H. Kawahara (Kyoto: Advanced Telecommunications Research Institute, 2002). For instance, for decades seismologists could chart earthquakes, tidal waves and volcanic eruptions, yet their resulting graphs looked too similar to predict which event was being described – it was only after the horrible aftermath that one could know. Dombois' use of audification, however, makes audible the differences between the effects.

14. Benjamin J. Vakoc, Ryan M. Lanning, James A. Tyrrell, Timothy P. Padera, Lisa A. Bartlett, Triantafyllos Stylianopoulos, Lance L. Munn, Guillermo J .Tearney, Dai Fukumura, Rakesh K. Jain, and Brett E. Bouma, "Threedimensional microscopy of the tumor microenvironment in vivo using optical frequency domain imaging," *Nature Medicine* 15 (2009): pp. 1219–1223, doi:10.1038/nm.1971.

15. Trevor Pinch and Karin Bijsterveld, eds., *The Oxford Handbook of Sound Studies* (Oxford: Oxford University Press, 2012), p. 552. Another example is Andrea Polli's *Atmospherics/Weather Works*, which uses a 15-channel sound system to recreate significant storms in the New York/Long Island area, etc. For more information see http://www.andreapolli.com/studio/atmospherics/.

16. https://vimeo.com/118346045.

17. Hopkins, in particular, with his paintings' alchemy-like use of volatile materials, also calls to mind many similar themes that Marcel Duchamp's *The Large Glass* unleashed and which *Delay* employs. I am indebted to Stefan Banz, the artist, Marcel Duchamp scholar and director of the KMD – Kunsthalle Marcel Duchamp, for pointing out this parallel.

18. Petr Kotik, *The Music of Marcel Duchamp*, CD liner notes to music by Marcel Duchamp (Berlin: Edition Block and Paula Cooper Gallery, 1991).

    In the turbulent years from 1912 to 1915, Marcel Duchamp, one of the most important artists of this century, worked with musical ideas. He composed two works of music and a conceptual piece – a note suggesting a musical happening . . . The third piece *Sculpture Musicale (Musical Sculpture)* is a note on a small piece of paper, which Duchamp also included in the *Green Box*. According to Arturo Schwarz, the piece was written sometime during 1912-1920/21, although 1913 is the most probable year. The *Musical Sculpture* is similar to the Fluxus pieces of the early 1960s. These works combine objects with performance, audio with visual, known and unknown factors, and elements explained and unexplained. A realization of such a piece can result in an event/happening, rather than a performance.

19. Stefan Banz, *Marcel Duchamp: Pharmacie* (Nuremberg: Verlag für moderne Kunst, 2013), p. 135.

    For Marcel Duchamp, his first major work was *La mariée mise a nu par ses célibataires, même*, also known as *Le grand verre* (*The Bride Stripped Bare by Her Bachelors, Even*, aka *The Large Glass*), a *retard en verre*. One of the ninety-four sheets of his *Boîte verte* reads: ". . . un retard en verre, comme on dirait un poème en prose ou un crachoir en argent" (a delay in glass, as you would say a poem in prose or a spittoon in silver). Duchamp thus underscores that time is one of the fundamental elements in the *Grand verre*: the Bride and her Bachelors wait endlessly and hopelessly for their desires to be satisfied. The deferment is impossible to bridge, unavoidably leading to sexual frustration.

    Retard en verre can also be read as a *retard envers*, a delayed, hesitant, or deferred reverse side. And in so doing, Duchamp's unusual addition is a subtle play on words that makes us attentive to the fact that the *Grand verre* is not just to be viewed from the front, but also has a reverse, and thus cannot only be seen from one perspective.

i. Marcel Duchamp, *Duchamp du signe*, ed. Michel Sanouillet (Paris: Flammarion, 1994), 41.

ii. See Paul Franklin in an interview with Merce Cunningham, in *Étant donné Marcel Duchamp*, no. 6 (2005), 8–19, here quoted in *Dancing Around the Bride: Cage, Cunningham, Johns, Rauschenberg, and Duchamp*, ed. Carlos Basualdo and Erica F. Battle (Philadelphia: Philadelphia Museum of Art, 2012), 263: "In his notes for the *Large Glass*, Duchamp described the *Large Glass* as a '*retard en verre*' or 'delay in glass'. Time is one of its fundamental elements. On the most basic level, the Bride and the Bachelors constantly wait to consummate their desire, which, of course, never happens. The delay is a perpetual one, signifying frustrated sexual desire."

Mary Sherman's Delay (in Collaboration with Florian Grond, 2015–2016), or the Audification of the Gaze

by Lorella Abenavoli

Translation from French by Ron Ross

Central to Mary Sherman's spare work are desire, synesthesia, and the scopic drive, and in this installation she posits the question: "What if you could hear a painting?" [1] *Delay* is a metaphor for desire, its deferral resonating in the title, whether manifest in the anticipation or after-the-fact. It suggests a melancholic approach to painting as itself the ever-fleeting object of desire. Painting is thus the beating heart of an installation in which sound floods the exhibition space. It is this continuum, with its technical implementation, straddling visual and auditory perception, that is the subject of this article. I give particular attention to the audification, which here disperses the painting acoustically throughout the gallery, touching our entire body. Audification, a type of sonification, consists of taking any non-audible data that can be captured and represented in the form of a wave and transforming it into sound. Electromagnetic or mechanical waves (also consisting of sound) may thus be audified, but one can also audify abstract data so long as its graphic representation can be deployed in the form of temporal curve within a Cartesian framework. For example, the graphed changes in a body's temperature can be given the form of an audio track in sound processing software and then processed acoustically. In *Delay*, Mary Sherman and Florian Grond explore a tactile audification that employs painting as its topographic source.

Though minimal in form, *Delay* is a relatively complex setup to describe. The kinetic and interactive installation occupies the entire gallery space [2] (see page 33). At the heart of the installation is a small, six-inch by six-inch, white, impasto oil painting hung at eye level (see page 25, figure 3). Situated in the middle of the gallery space, turned away from the wall a few feet back, it levitates within an aluminum frame held by supports anchored on the ground and on the ceiling (see figure 1). The painting is lit by a projection that casts a clear shadow of the entire orthogonal structure onto the wall. When spectators pass before the lit beam, they create an eclipse that obscures the painting; the action is reinforced by a blind that pivots around to block the painting out altogether. This aluminum blind, however, has five small rectangular shutters that slowly slide out to let

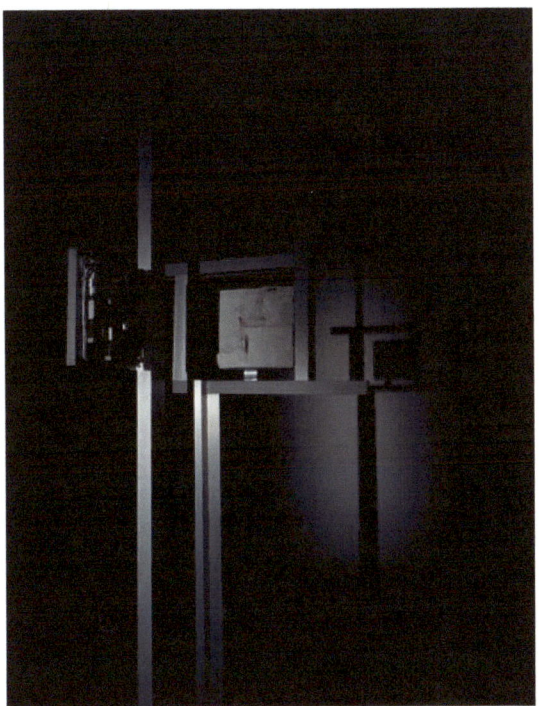

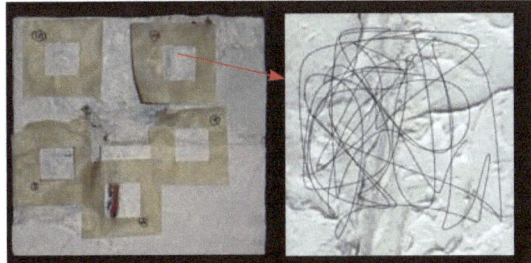

Figure 1 is a detail of *Delay* in the 'start' position, showing the mechanism (on the aluminum plate to the left) that opens and closes (like shutters) once the plate is positioned in front of the painting.

Figure 2 depicts one of the gaze-like trajectories that Grond audified.

MARY SHERMAN'S DELAY (IN COLLABORATION WITH FLORIAN GROND, 2015–2016), OR THE AUDIFICATION OF THE GAZE

in a beam that illuminates a small portion of painting surface, revealing only fragments as they open (see page 31). Each of these painting fragments is then audified and played back in the space in tandem with its slow exposure, giving rise to mineral sounds having crystalline resonances. The five speakers that disseminate the sound of each audification are incorporated into their separate white monochrome frames and hung on the walls surrounding the device described above, thus playing on the spatialization of the sound sources. As the cycle of shutter openings and sounded audifications comes to an end, the blind opens to reveal the painting once more, until the next visitor triggers a new cycle.

The sonification of each painting fragment was produced from its topographic data, reconstructed with the help of a medical imaging tomographic scanner,[3] the two-dimensional, black and white representations of which were then given to Grond. He then used parameter mapping sonification to produce a hybrid audification from samples of topographical relief data. Parameter mapping sonification is another type of sonification, which consists of attributing sound values to data without there being a mimetic relationship with the source material, as there is in audification. Grond envisaged the sonification of *Delay* as the audible trace of one's gaze as it sweeps over the painting. "I invented a line on this surface that sweeps across it like one's gaze does across a painting" (Grond, 2016).[4] (See figure 2.) The audification thus consisted of "tracing" a wandering line on the surface of this fragment of painting, very much like our own gaze. Technically, this line "profiles" the painting, tracing it in order to make it audible (see page 29, figure 8). Just as the grooves in a vinyl disk resemble a topography of valleys, the profile of rifts in the painting becomes a curve, which is then transposed into a sound curve, programmed to be read by software, thus constituting the audification in this work. Besides the application of these derivations, Grond applied some effects to the topographical data: depth was expressed as reverberation (thinned out for high points, accentuated for low ones); audio synthesis that suggests linguistic vowel formants was applied to nuances in color. The application here of these effects to two of the painting's topographical parameters actualizes the parameter mapping sonification. That said, audification remains predominant and, thanks to their indicial relationship with the painting, the sounds in *Delay* suggest a very concrete auditory image of its surface. Sound here becomes medium, in the formal sense of the term, and we "really" hear the rubbing of the pictorial surface, allowing us to indeed hear painting [5] at the moment that it disappears from our field of vision.

Sherman says of her work: "*Delay* is a spare installation about impossible love. It is meant to be a lure: to be seen, heard (…) and experienced; to delay people, as love does — which, in this case, stems from my love of painting (…)" [6] This work embodies the image of desire, whose object, the painting, vanishes as soon as one approaches it. The mythical elements of painting are set before us: the shadow cast on the wall recalls the story recounted by Pliny the Elder,[7] in which the daughter of legendary potter Butades draws the shadow of her departing lover on the wall. Based on the absent lover, this myth is said to tell of the origin of painting, the subject of Sherman's work. The blind that masks the painting at least as surely as our shadow cast on the wall is unquestionably an impediment to our scopic drive, the expression of desire, which is nonetheless conveyed by the aurality of the painting's audification. Coinciding with the unfolding sound, the shutter's slow opening engenders a caress, an optical tactility of which sound is the medium. Audification thus augments an impaired vision by proposing a sensory alternative. The tactile function of the gaze is replaced by the haptic emanation of sound that traverses the air and connects us with the work. We perceive the painting thanks to the sound that pervades the space. The audification enables the painting to literally touch us as the device enacts a technological synesthesia.

REFERENCES AND NOTES

1. The question is posed as such at the start of the video presentation of the artist's work on her website: http://transculturalexchange.org/marysherman/works/current/delay/vd.html, accessed May 17, 2016.

2. The description is based on the exhibition held at Galleri KiT, Norwegian University of Science and Technology, Trondheim, Norway, 2014 (Curator: Regina Moeller). See http://www.kit.ntnu.no/en/content/delay-exhibition-opening-talk-mary-sherman-florian-grond, accessed May 14, 2016.

3. The device is mentioned in the introductory text for the exhibition, which was held in Trondheim; *ibid.*, accessed March 15, 2016.

4. Phone interview with Lorella Abenavoli and Florian Grond, conducted January 27, 2016.

5. While there has never been any actual contact with the painting, only calculations based on coordinates on the surface of the canvas, the audification virtually reconstructs a chafing of the painting's relief.

6. Excerpt from Mary Sherman's website: http://transculturalexchange.org/marysherman/works/current/delay/vd.html, accessed January 25, 2016.

7. Pliny the Elder, *The Natural History* XXXV (c. 77 A.D.), § 151 and 152.

The (Un)Green Box

Wooden box containing electronics, drawings, scans and maquettes of various sizes

13" × 13" × 4"

Edition: 5

2015–2016

DESCRIPTION

Each edition of *The (Un)Green Box* [1] has roughly the same dimensions as the speakers created for the kinetic installation *Delay*. Inside are the models, drawings, scientific scans and other archival materials that went into the making of that work. Additionally – a bit like a music box – when the last item is removed from each, it triggers the sounds generated by one of the five scanned areas of the painting used in *Delay*. In other words, the boxes are also speakers. In this way, then, each box is visually the same, [2] but aurally fragmented. It takes all five boxes to access *Delay*'s full array of sounds.

Delay was meant, in part, to show that a painting is more than a static visual object – that it is also a record of time passing (made apparent through its sonification) and more. *The (Un)Green Box* extends this idea. It also, like *Delay*, purposely references a work by Marcel Duchamp – in this case, *The Bride Stripped Bare by her Bachelors, Even (The Green Box)*. Similar to that work, *The (Un)Green Box* suggests that despite the fact that *Delay* appeals to various senses like sight, sound and, indirectly, touch, it should not be understood on "retinal" or any other sensory terms alone.

ACKNOWLEDGEMENTS

Marc Fournel for the boxes' fabrication.

REFERENCES AND NOTES

1. *The UnGreen Box* was created in collaboration with Florian Grond, who contributed his expertise, speakers and audification for the piece.

2. In reality, the sketches and notes for each edition differ slightly from one to another as they were hand-copied and, hence, prone to variation.

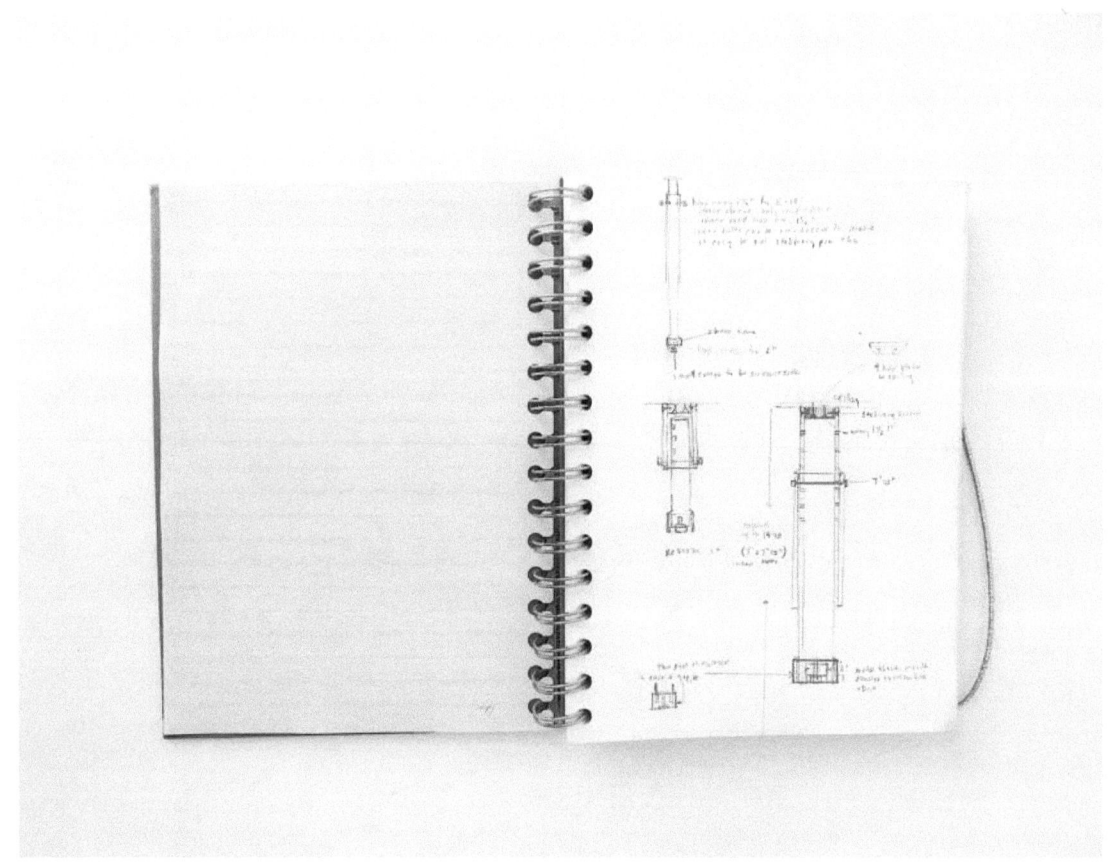

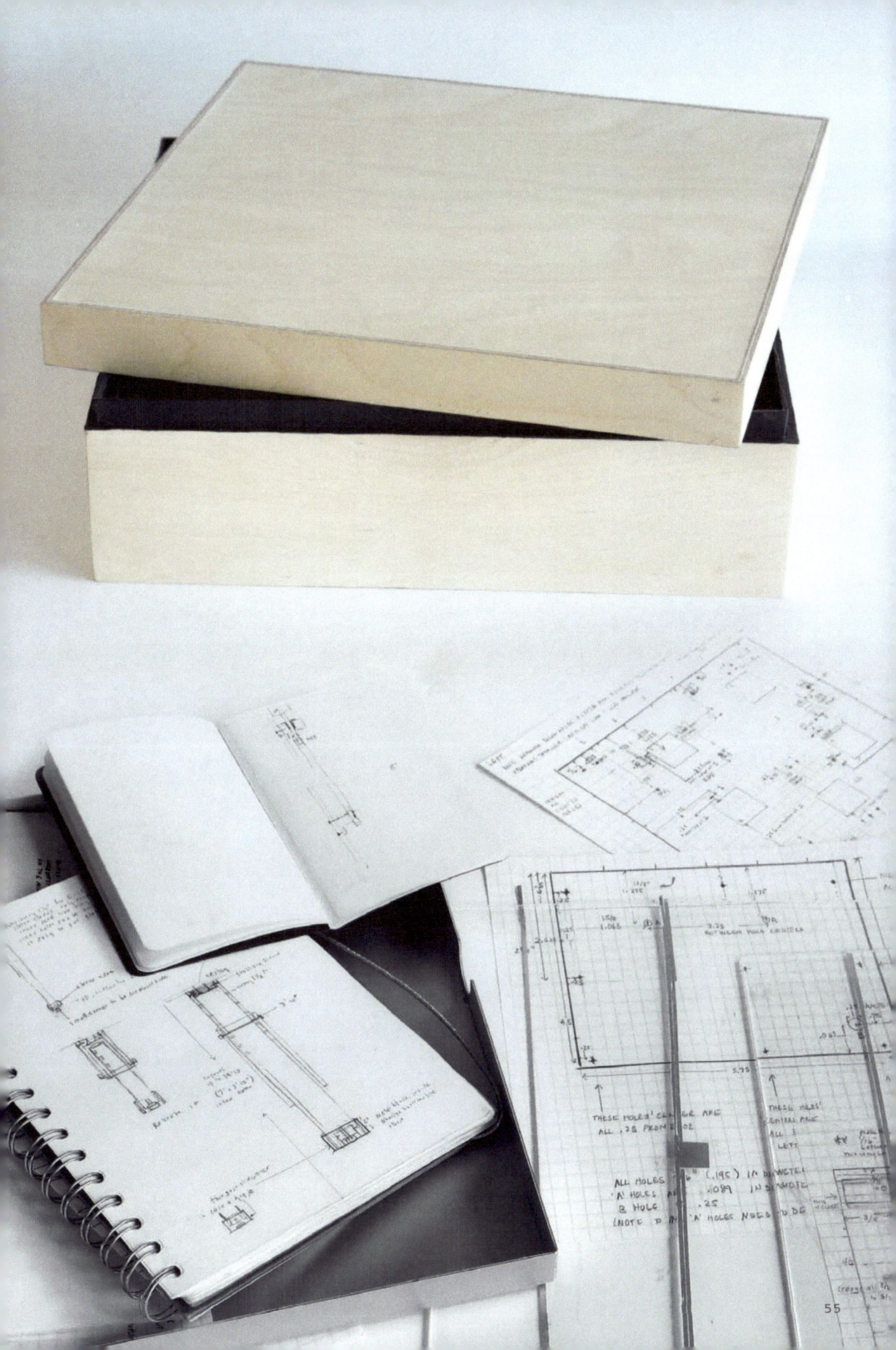

DREAMING

Eri, After Dark

Sound (by Benoit Granier), ribbon, magnet, wooden box, ink on paper (doubling as a speaker membrane), motors, star LEDs, sound module, aluminum and microprocessor

10" × 10" × 6"

2011–2012 (re-programmed 2015)

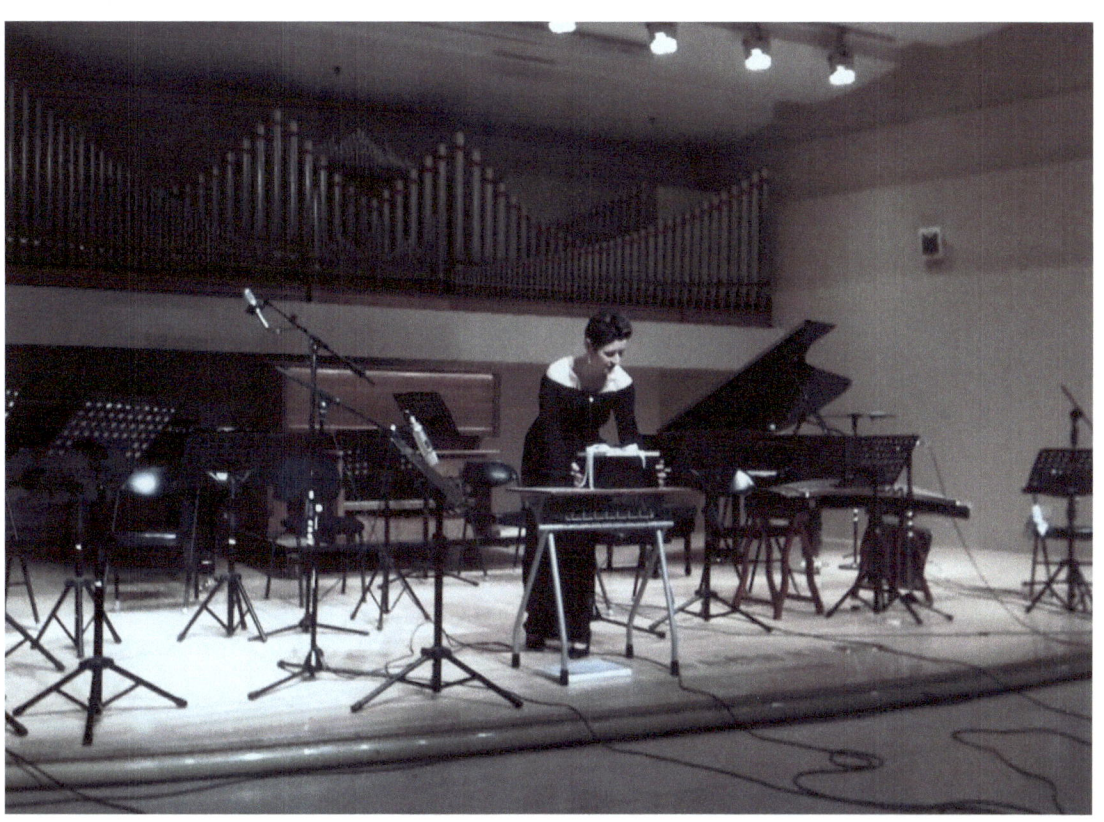

DESCRIPTION

Inspired by and made for Benoit Granier's musical composition "Eri," [1] this piece was originally constructed to be easily transported to China, where it first "performed" as part of a live, electro-acoustic concert at the Beijing Conservatory in February 2012.

Brought on stage, like a present tied with a bow, *Eri, After Dark* is then unwrapped: The top, a Chinese-style ink painting, is placed standing off to one side while a magnet from a matching jewel case triggers a hidden reed switch, which activates the piece. The flaps of the box then open one after another so that, after the first one opens, the sound module is triggered. Once all the flaps are opened, the box's content is revealed as an intense, Pandora-like light (created by a cluster of LEDs mounted inside). The piece then continues to transmit Granier's composition through the ink painting/speaker until the next-to-the-last flap closes. Afterwards, the final flap closes as well, and the piece is carried off stage. [2]

ACKNOWLEDGEMENTS

George Bossarte for programming assistance.

PERFORMANCE VENUES

Drive-By Projects, *Eri, After Dark*, Boston, MA, 2016

King Seattle Station, *9e2 (9 Evenings: Theatre & Engineering, a Commemorative Festival)*, Seattle, WA, 2016

New York University's Loewe Theater, *Electrified Data*, 2015

Beijing Central Conservatory of Music, *On Native Music*, Beijing, China (organized by Benoit Granier), 2012

EXHIBITION VENUE

Beijing Forestry University, *X-Dialogue*, Part 2, Beijing, China, 2012

RELATED TALKS

Sound, Images and Data Conference, New York University, May 2015

Inbetween, Norwegian University of Science and Technology, Trondheim, Norway, 2014

PRESS

Aceti, Lanfranco. "Electrified Data." *Rhizome*, July 23, 2015. Accessed August 10, 2016. http://classic.rhizome.org/announce/events/61515/view/.

"The Agenda: This Week in New York." *Art in America*, July 21, 2015.

REFERENCES AND NOTES

1. "Eri" is an interlude from Granier's opera *Eri, After Dark*, based on Haruki Murakami novel of the same title. The opera follows the life of Murakami's fictional sisters Mari and Eri in Tokyo, where Eri is lost between two worlds – the real one she is trying to escape and the fantasy one, where she is imprisoned within a television, waiting for her sister to retrieve her.

2. Untied and with the speaker/ink painting off to one side, the piece also can be presented as a freestanding sculpture, re-programmed to be activated by a sensor to open/close at pre-set times.

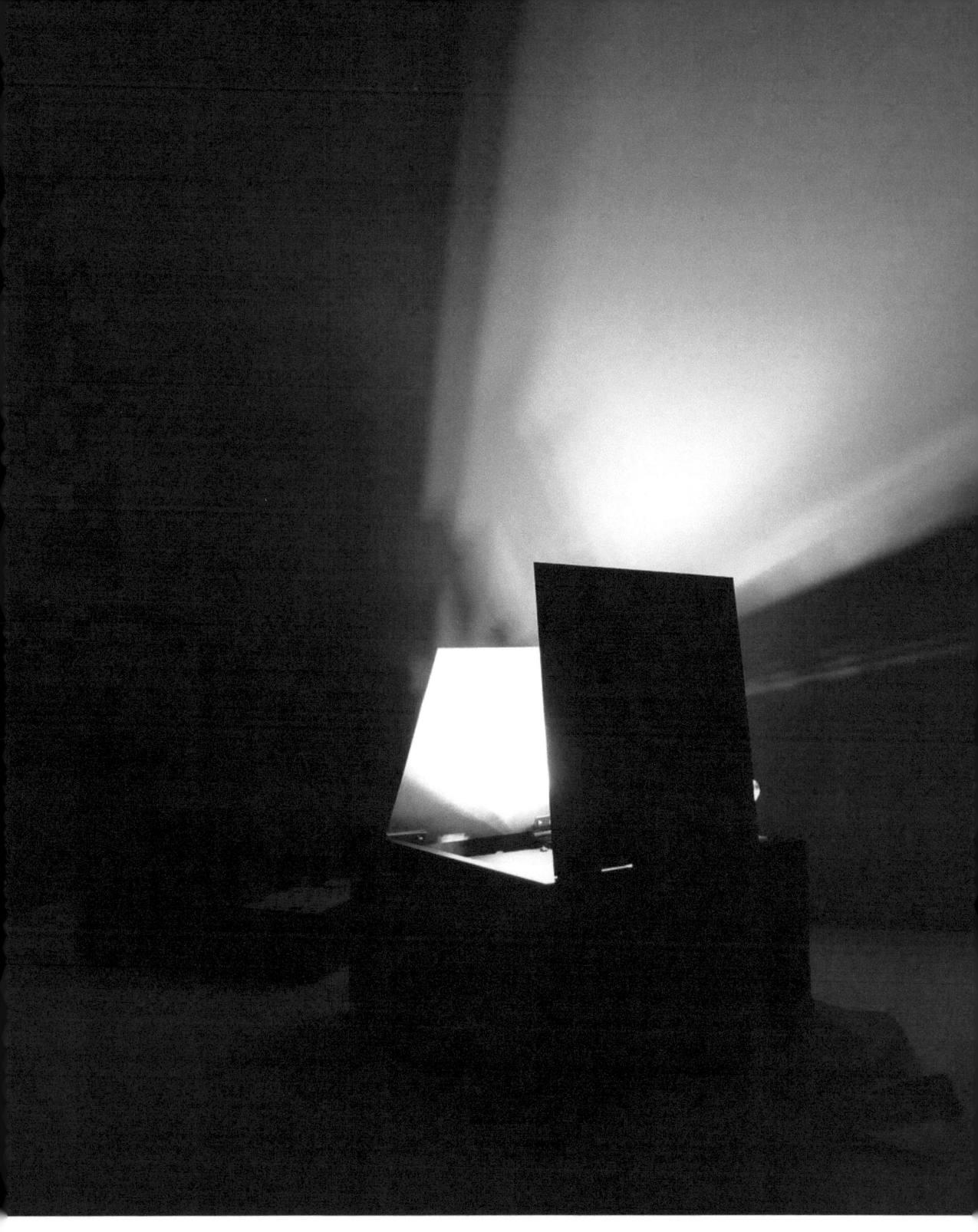

Eri, After Dark in performance at the Drive-By Gallery, 2016.
(Wall shadows intentionally created by the piece.)

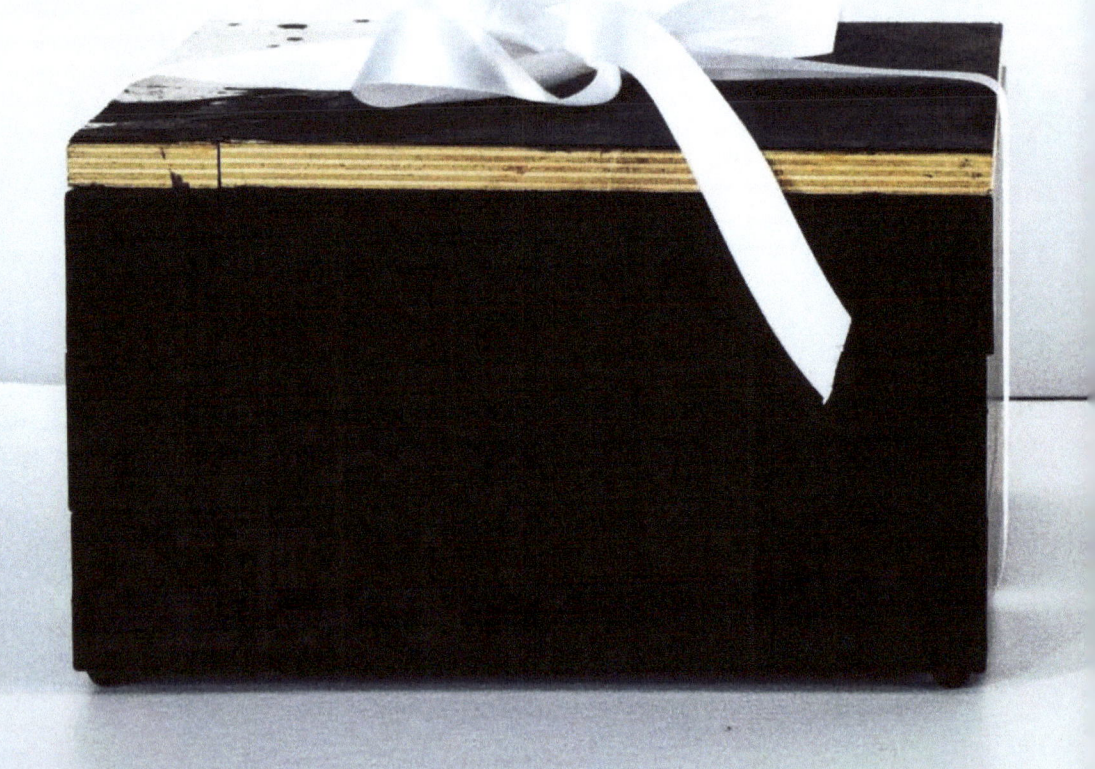

The Demise of a Dream, or Paradise Regained

by Mary Sherman

LOCATION/CURRENT CONTEXT

At the moment, the *Demise of a Dream, or Paradise Regained* exists only as a model [1] – a dream, if you will. Scaled up and sited, it can be located anywhere: a region suffering from urban blight, a suburban vista, a city already replete with monuments and architectural jewels or even in a remote dessert location or atop a barge, adrift in the middle of the ocean. [2] All of these areas have qualities for which the proposed piece would be well suited: in the first case, the *Demise of a Dream* would have the power of attracting new businesses and, thus, providing economic relief. In the tranquil suburbs, it would offer a break from the usual routine (but not too upsetting of one, as it has its own routine as well). And, in those locations already chock-full of structural wonders, it would be the next wunderkind on the block – complete with technological advances, including walls that act as transducers [3] and a programmable kinetic roof. (Again, see footnote 1.) And, sited in a remote location, it would have the power to become the perfect foil for a pilgrimage; a new *Spiral Jetty*, *Cadillac Ranch* or wistful World Fair has-been. [4]

Like all buildings – in all the cases above – *Demise of a Dream, or Paradise Regained* is conjured out of desire. But it is also more: built into it is its realization and its demise (or, Process and Methodology of Removal). A new dream will inevitably take its place (see The Resultant Condition). So it has been, and so it will remain. Human beings appear thus programmed.

MISSION STATEMENT

It begins with a dream. Every building starts out as a hope and only in time does it turn into an office, monument, home or, as Roxy Music so blithely croons, a heartache.

The grandest dreams are often the most targeted; eventually taken down by a warring state, industry's greed or their own hubris. What was once the tallest building is replaced almost as soon as it is built. The jubilation subsides; and eventually nature and man take their toll and demolition is not far behind. But the dream remains. What is demolished is only the structure's physical mass.

The *Demise of a Dream, or Paradise Regained* embodies that dream in a tangible form. It is the Genie in the Bottle, Pandora's Box, the Monolith at the end of *2001: A Space Odyssey*. Its power lays in wait until just the right moment, then it slowly takes shape and rises to the sky (with fanfare, of course). [5] And when finally unfolded/erected, it is clear that it contains only an intense light, a kind of magical promise that reaches up to the heavens – timed to do so, every night, just a few moments after the sun slips behind the horizon. And then it closes. (The total duration of the complete "performance" is just under 8 minutes, well within the maximum sustained attention span of a typical person.) This goes on for days.

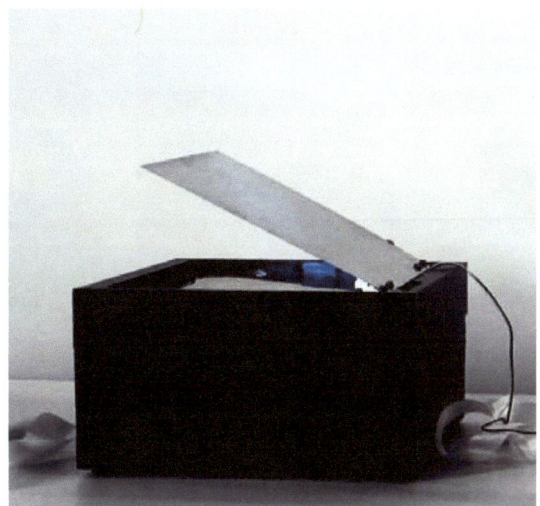

The structure becomes a tourist attraction. New businesses open up nearby to take advantage of its popularity. The press gushes over it; the public comes to gawk. But over time, even this magic fades: the spectacle becomes commonplace, the dream turns sour and it shuts down. It has satiated the public's imagination. In the past, like most prefabbed structures, it could easily have been hauled off to another place to dazzle new audiences. But we have become so used to experiencing so much virtually that the need to experience a real presence can no longer justify such an expense. Instead, it could lie there, collapsed like the globe from the New York World's Fair, in a place that couldn't sustain the economy it once attracted. But nature (of which we are part) abhors a vacuum. In no time, the void would certainly be transformed (see The Resultant Condition). The possibilities are endless. The structure's former opening to the heavens will become a vague memory and even that will slowly die. A few pictures will remain. People will talk wistfully about the time when... meanwhile new dreams will have supplanted it. For dreams cannot be demolished. After all, dreams are the stuff of which we are made; it was only Hope that Pandora was able to keep from escaping from her ill-opened Box.

NOTE

The work is, perhaps, best understood, viewed and heard in the video. [3] There, it can be seen that the sound is broadcast via a transducer mounted to the lid of the model, so that the ink painting on top functions as a speaker membrane. For *Demise of a Dream, or Paradise Regained* parts of the structure's walls would serve the same function, so that the building would literally play the sound composed for it.

THE DEMISE OF A DREAM, OR PARADISE REGAINED

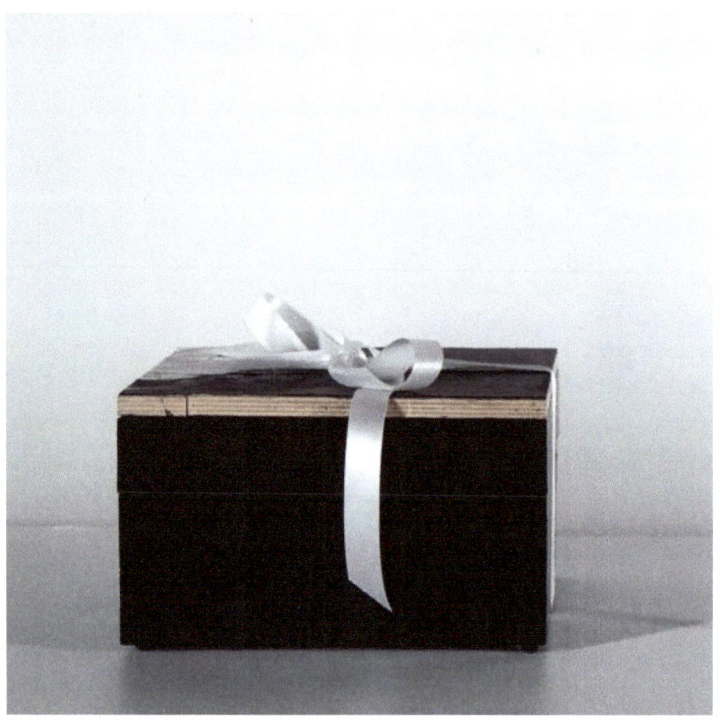

Awaiting the Ribbon Cutting Ceremony
Note: The structure is purposely presented against a blank background. (See Location/Context and The Resultant Condition for further explanation.)

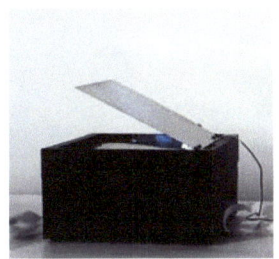 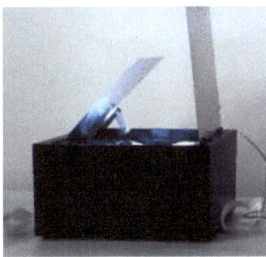 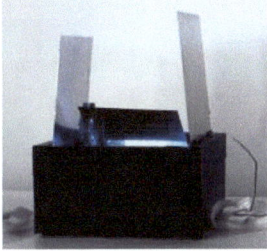 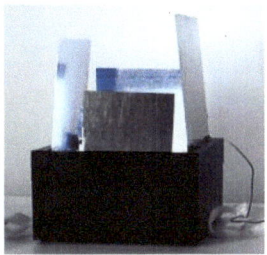

The Prelude (to the Current Context, or
the Building is first Revealed)

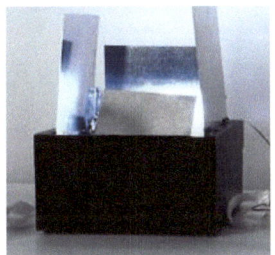 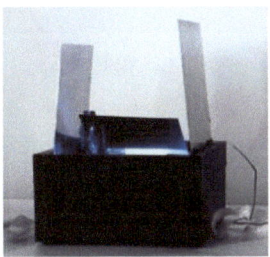 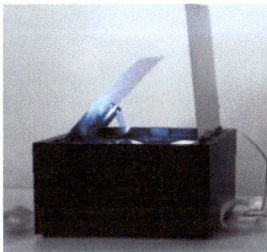 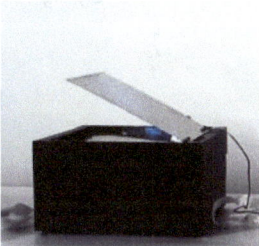

Location/Context
Act 1: The Dream Revealed, or the Building is Erected for the First and Subsequent Times
(See Mission Statement for more details.)

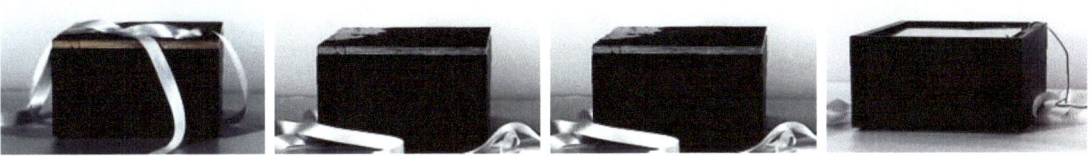

The Process and Methodology of Removal
Act 2: The Demise of a Dream, or The Taking Down of a Building
(i.e. The Last Closure. See Mission Statement for more information.)

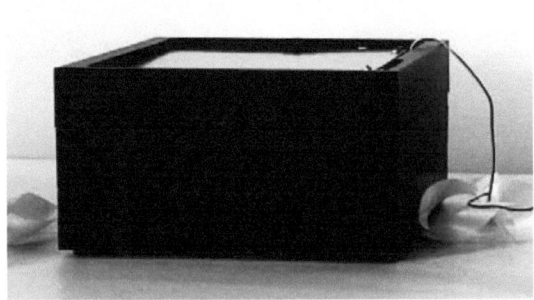

The Resultant Condition

Act 3: Paradise Regained

The building has closed for the last time. People are tired of its spectacle and clamors for something "useful" have arisen. *The Demise of a Dream, or Paradise Regained*'s escapist appeal has gone by the same wayside as art programs in public schools. But the void only remains as such for a short time. . . .

New dreams are in hot pursuit. [7] Among these: an elevator could be inserted into the structure's interior to take people up to the flat surface of its now-collapsed sides. With turf placed on top, the elevated box becomes a park with USB ports for people to broadcast their own soundtracks. In colder regions and times, it could become an outdoor skating rink. Or, just by cutting a door into the front, a new techno nightclub could emerge, or even a shelter for the homeless. (The outer walls' former gearing would now be either attraction's hallmark allure.) If first erected in the Arctic, it could be left adrift as a landing pad for migrating birds, or a raft for polar bears when their icebergs melt. In the desert, it could become a stage for the next Woodstock. The possibilities are as endless as our need to define space.

REFERENCES AND NOTES

1. https://vimeo.com/152135482?utm_source=email&utm_medium=vimeo-cliptranscode-201504&utm_campaign=29220

2. It can be solar powered and, hence, could survive in any of these locations.

3. The sound that the structure plays (triggered by an interior sound module, which is set off by the ceremonial removal of its flat roof – hence, the ribbon in the initial image) is Benoit Granier's *Eri, After Dark*, which was composed specifically for this piece. *Eri, After Dark* was inspired by Haruki Murakami's novel of the same title, in which Eri is lost between two worlds – the real one she is trying to escape and the fantasy one in which she is imprisoned within a television set – not unlike what we all experience today: a world brought to us via digitally compressed means (visual, aural and kinetic simulacra) that mimic reality, sometimes even convincing us that they are as real as reality.

   The Demise of a Dream, or Paradise Regained will likely suffer this same fate. It is highly possible that its existence may never surpass the model phase. Even if the wind-shear factors were solved and it was realized on a scale that could be duplicated or transported (like any pre-fab building), its sure-to-be–publicized, outdoor appearance would certainly kill off any desire to move it elsewhere. Through widespread print and virtual press coverage, Selfies and the like, people would already feel that they know the building without the need to experience it first hand. Its first real-world incarnation is, thus, doomed to be its last. Still the point remains: Another will inevitably follow.

4. The model shown in the video exists and when closed is roughly 10" x 10" x 6". It can be scaled up to a variety of site requirements. A scale of 1"=15' (well within the maximum, modular transport size) would allow it to be driven to any location and (being self-contained and powered by generators or solar cells) be ready for 'display' within hours of its arrival. For example, this situation would be ideal in a remote location, as the piece's arrival could then be incorporated as part of its mythical appeal. On the other hand, a scale of 1"=250' – roughly the equivalent of the width and a third of the length of a Manhattan block – would be appropriate for a larger city. And, in this case, a suitable waiting period – to build anticipation – should be considered before the first day of the building's opening/erection.

5. Transducers would be attached to the walls so that they double as speaker membranes.

6. As previously explained, and as the video link and stills above reveal, *Demise of a Dream, or Paradise Regained* represents a dream; therefore, it mysteriously appears like a present. Its erection and taking down – its complete lifecycle – are built into its package, as is its ultimate demise and resurrection. (See *The Resultant Condition/ Act 3: Paradise Regained*.)

7. Instead of creating Photoshop montages of the possibilities suggested above, I have left the structure – as in the beginning – depicted against a blank, indeterminate surrounding so that no singular "dream" is suggested and, thus, takes hold of the reader's/viewer's imagination. Instead, all dreams are possible.

WAITING

Waiting for Yves

Sound (by Yannick Franck), French ultramarine oil bar, rosin paper, nine red lights (two mechanically altered), ticket machine, embossed and engraved "tickets" (with quotes from Samuel Beckett's *Waiting for Godot*) and sound isolating headphones with mp3 players

Dimensions variable

Video documentation: https://vimeo.com/111466726

2010–2011

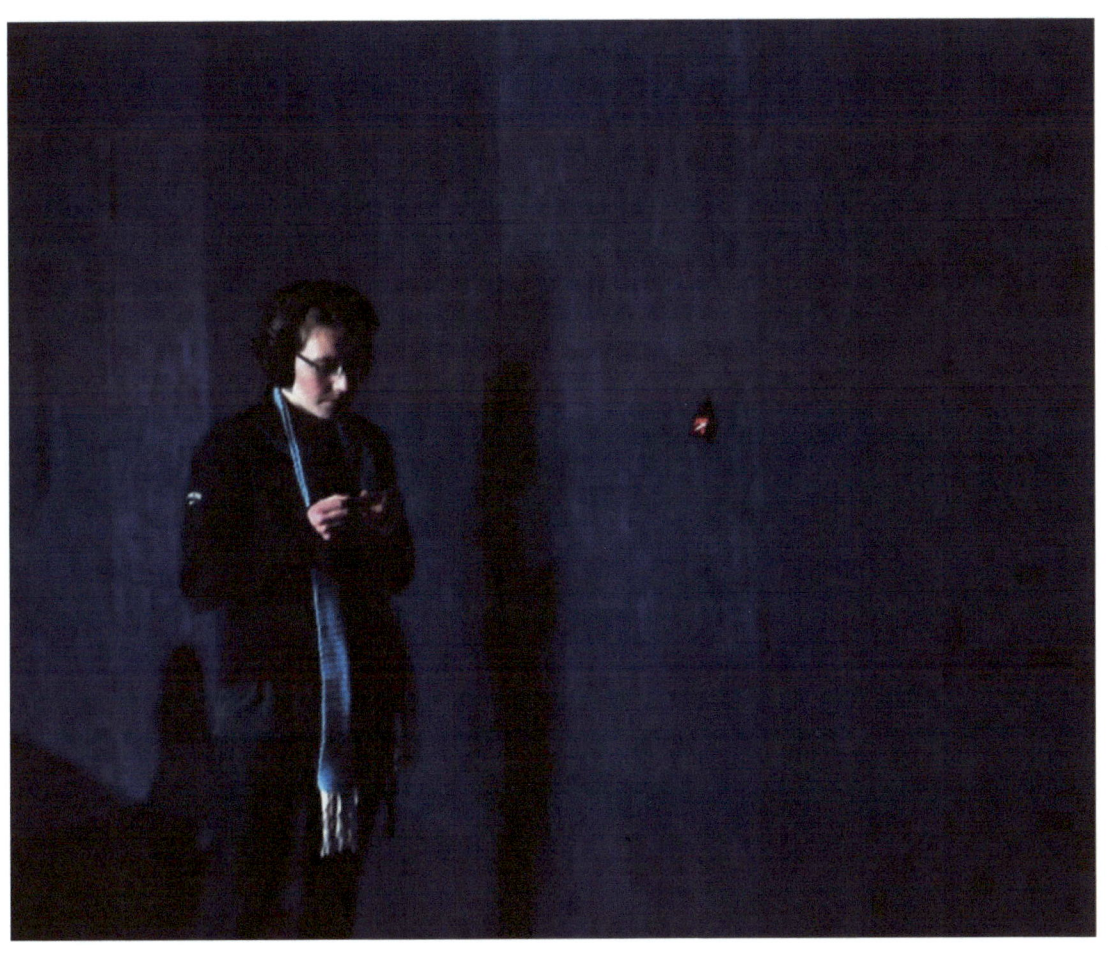

WAITING FOR YVES

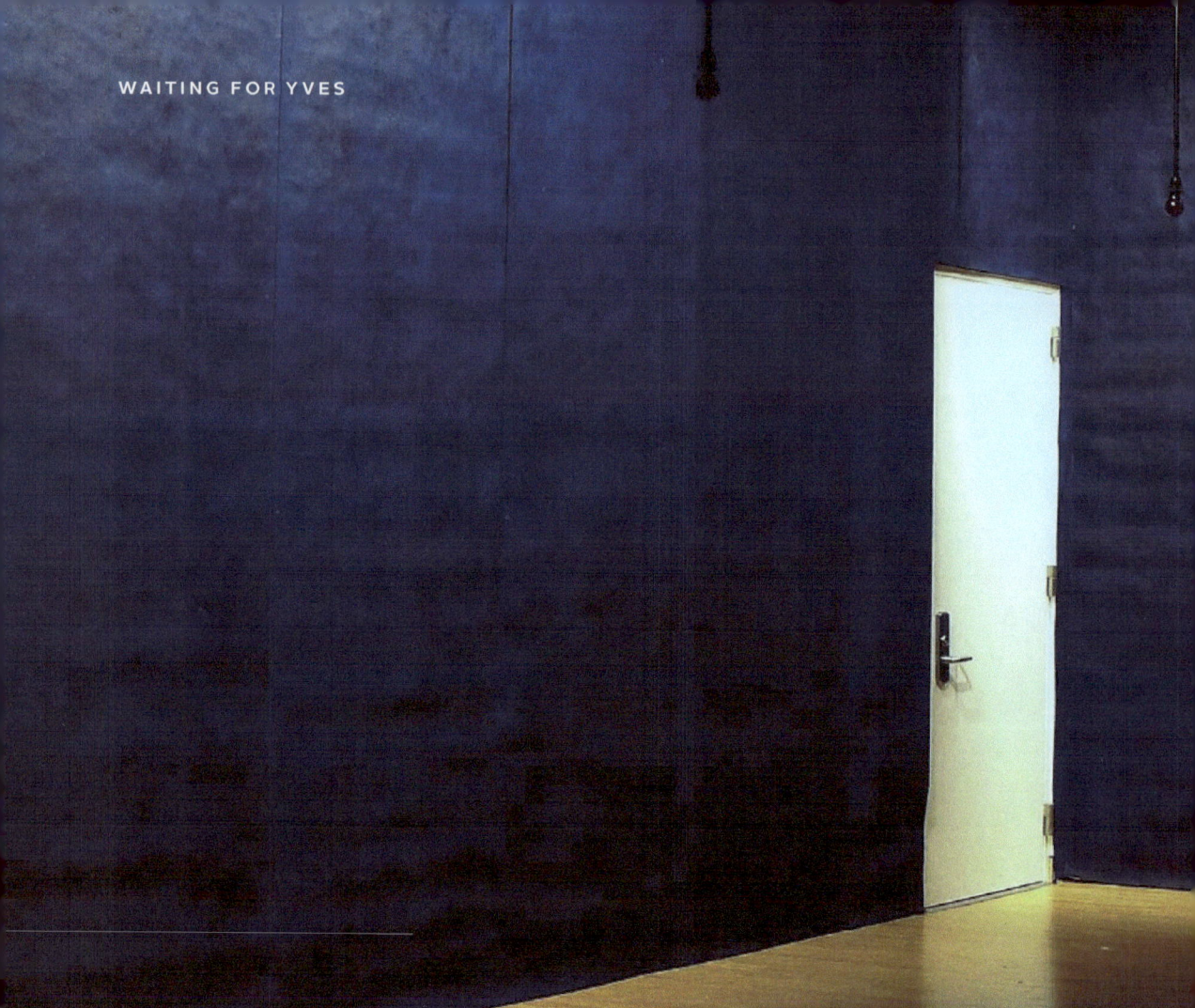

DESCRIPTION

Waiting for Yves is a surround-sound painting. It includes a soundtrack – Yannick Franck's haunting trek through snow *Vaihessa* (accessed through mobile, sound isolating headphones) – and a room lined with rosin paper, covered by thousands upon thousands of strokes of French ultramarine oil bar. From the ceiling hang nine red lights, two of which dim and brighten so slowly as to be almost imperceptible. The only other thing that punctuates the room is a string of tickets, sticking out from a hole in one of the walls, alternately embossed in text and braille with Samuel Beckett's famous lines, "I can't go on"; "I will go on."

Waiting for Yves was created to take painting out of its historically frame-bound constraints into the realm of space, time and sound. Like in a cyclorama, its audience steps into the piece, leaving the real world behind and walking into another. The work both purposely references Yves Klein's *Le Vide (The Specialization of Sensibility in the Raw Material State into Stabilized Pictorial Sensibility, The Void)* and creates an intimate sound environment in which – as in Beckett's *Waiting for Godot* – the situation is pregnant with possibility, vast seeming nothingness and the realization that one must just go on.

ACKNOWLEDGEMENTS

Walter Lenk for the lighting circuitry and Grace Chen and Jonathan Talit for paper production assistance.

EXHIBITION VENUES

OBORO (as part of *Dream Mechanics/Mécaniques oniriques*), Montreal, Canada, curated by Tamar Tembeck, 2016

Crafton Hills College, Yucaipa, CA, curated by Snezana Petrovic, 2015

Boston Sculptors Gallery, Boston, MA, 2011

PRESS

Hoffman, Donna. "Art Gallery Hosts Work of Renowned Artist." *Colton City News*, March 14, 2015.

McQuaid, Cate. "Material Worlds." *The Boston Globe*, October 19, 2011.

RELATED TALKS

Crafton Hills College, Yucaipa, CA, February 17 and 19, 2015

Untitled (Drawing)

French ultramarine oil bar on rosin paper

36" × 3600"

1993

DESCRIPTION

The work consists of thousands upon thousands of strokes of blue oil bar on rosin paper. This piece was originally made – like many of the pre-mechanized works – both to be reconfigured and to serve as yet another variation on the questioning of traditional definitions of artistic media (in this case, drawing). Here, the work is shown on the floor. In other instances, it has been draped over a stairway or, in still others, pinned to a wall with the remainder falling down over the floor below. Later, many more such sheets were made as part of *Waiting for Yves*.

EXHIBITION VENUES

Mills Gallery, Boston Center for the Arts, Boston, MA, *The Drawing Show*, 1993

Hastahana tekija Mesudia, Kacuni, Bosnia and Herzegovina, permanent collection

PRESS

Alexander, M. Darsie. "The Drawing Show." *The South End News*, September 9, 1993.

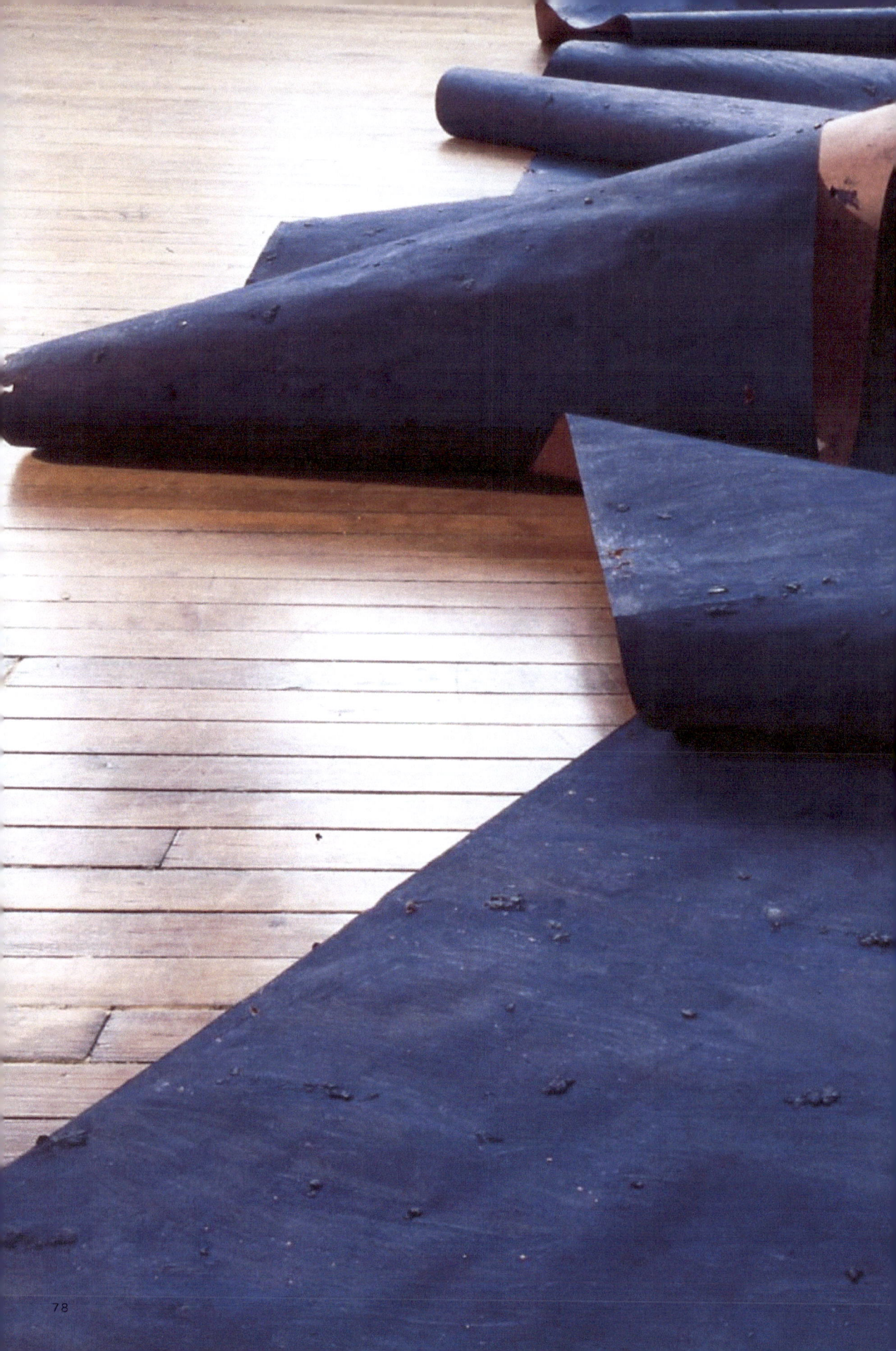

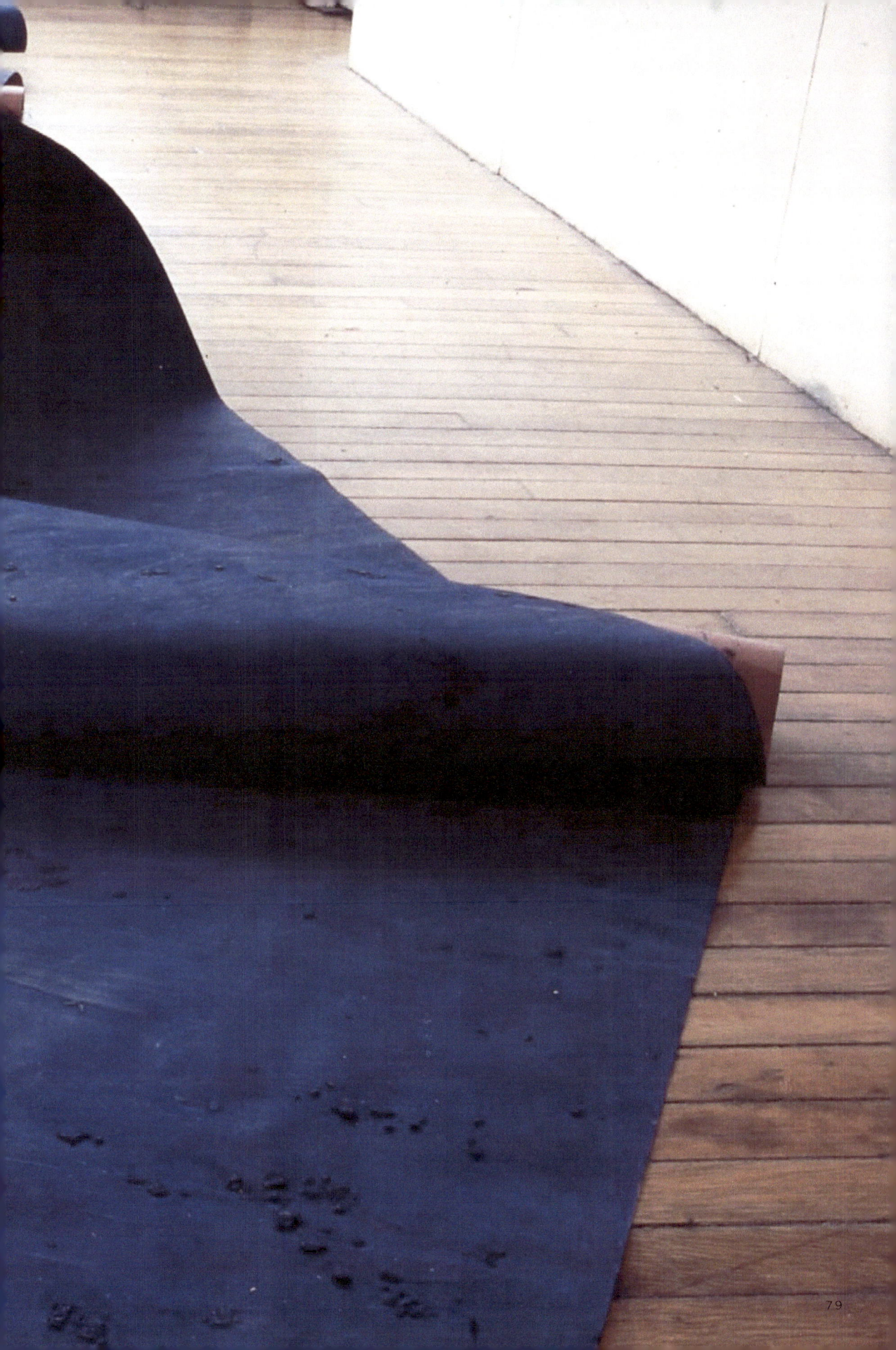

For Thomas

Ink, embossed and engraved "tickets" (with quotes from Samuel Beckett's *Waiting for Godot*)

Unlimited edition

1" × 600"

2015

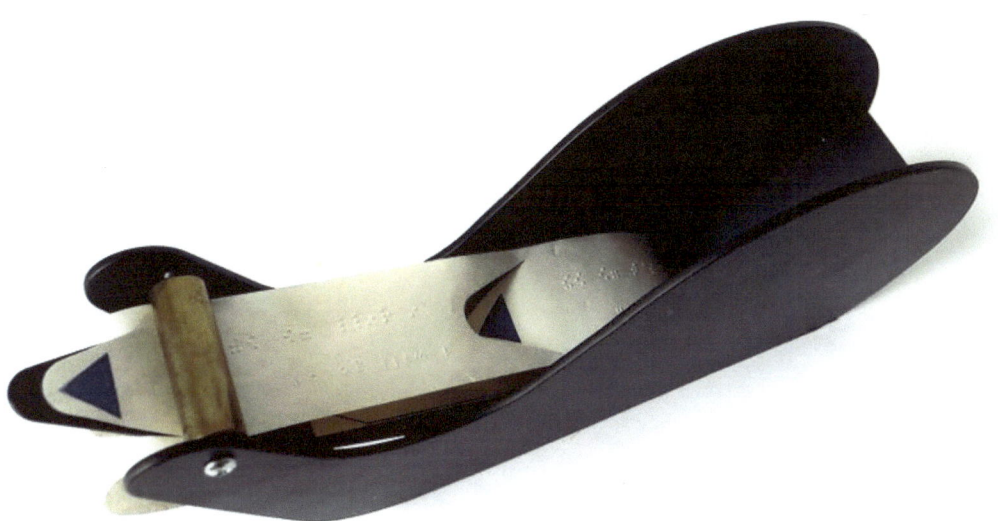

DESCRIPTION

This work was given to Thomas Trummer for *Views on Mainz*, [1] his departing exhibition from Kunsthalle Mainz. It consists of a deli-like dispenser containing one of the *Waiting for Yves'* rolls of tickets, alternatingly embossed in text and braille with "I can't go on"; "I will go on" from Beckett's *Waiting for Godot*.

EXHIBITION VENUE

Kunsthalle Mainz, Germany, *Views on Mainz*, 2015

FOR THOMAS

REFERENCES AND NOTES

1. Thomas Trummer, *Views on Mainz*, Kunsthalle Mainz, Germany, 2015, press release:

   111 Artists in One Office
   Opening: March 23, 2016, 7 pm
   Closing date to be determined

   With works by Nicole Ahland / Nevin Aladağ / Maria Anwander / Heike Aumüller / Josef Bauer / Marc Bauer / Lothar Baumgarten / Thomas Bayrle / Anne Berning / Johanna Billing / Monica Bonvicini / Brandstifter / Kerstin Brätsch / Andrea Büttner / Daniele Buetti / Tom Burr / Gerad Byrne / Ernst Caramelle / David Claerbout / Attila Csörgő / Edith Dekyndt / Anna Dot / Nils Dräger / Björn Drenkwitz / Heinrich Dunst / Uroš Đurić / Anne Eggebert / Stephan Engelke / Samuel Fath / Vadim Fishkin / Frank Gabriel / Rainer Ganahl / Susann Gassen / Agnès Geoffray / Harald Gfader / Nicola Goedecker / Polly Gould / Tamara Grcic / Sofia Greff / Sabine Groß / Katharina Grosse / Sandra Heinz / Nina Heinzel / Marc von der Hocht / Nikolas Hönig / Anne Hoffmann / Sofia Hultén / I. Helen Jilavu / Sven Johne / Franz Kapfer / Dieter Kiessling / Oliver Kelm / Herwig Kempinger / Esther Kläs / Jakob Lena Knebl / Peter Kogler / Anton Kokl / Claudia Larcher / Marko Lehanka / Sonia Leimer / Sara Masüger / Christian Mayer / Gerhard Meerwein / Ilka Meyer / Sarah Mock / Matt Mullican / João Onofre / Daniel Pauselius / Goran Petercol / Peter Piller / Emilie Pitoiset / August Priebe / Florian Pumhösl / Tobias Putrih / Katja von Puttkamer / Max Reintgen / Cornelia Rößler / Michael Sailstorfer / Judith Samen / Hans Schabus / Benjamin Schaefer / Markus Schinwald / Erik Schmelz / Marten Georg Schmid / Thomas Schmidt / Martin Schwenk / Mary Sherman / Six & Petritsch / John Skoog / Slavs and Tatars / Margherita Spiluttini / Friedemann von Stockhausen / Stoll & Wachall / Bernd Thewes / Sabine Tress / Stephan Truschel / Anna-Lena Tsutsui / Upper Bleistein / Gediminas Urbonas / Winfried Virnich / Simon Wachsmuth / Markus Walenzyk / Christoph Weber / Lisa Weber / Peter Weibel / Jonas Weichsel / Lois Weinberger / Anna Witt / Leo Wörner / Bruno Zhu / Heimo Zobernig

   The offices at galleries and museums fall into a different category from the exhibition space. They are working areas for everyday bureaucracy and organization, with neither high insurance or real estate values, nor any aura or discursive meaning. However, spatial hierarchies become more flexible during periods of transition. This, therefore, is an invitation to rediscover space and art. As my tenure as director of the Kunsthalle Mainz comes to an end – and before my successor moves in – I have transformed my office into a temporary exhibition. The furniture in my office has been temporarily removed, creating space for objects from artists' workshops to be put on display by Erik Schmelz.

   The types of items exhibited are random. This "collection" embellishes the conventional concept of art and takes a gentle poke at canonized ways of perceiving it. It is about condensed forms and purported use, about improvisation and personal vedute, the forgotten and the outcast and, not least, about a trove of souvenirs, thoughts, and stories.

Nocturne

Sound (by Yannick Franck), oil paint, polished aluminum, microprocessor, sound module, circuitry and motors

Track: variable; individual moving parts: 5½" × 11" × 5½"

Video documentation: https://vimeo.com/122215187

2007–2008

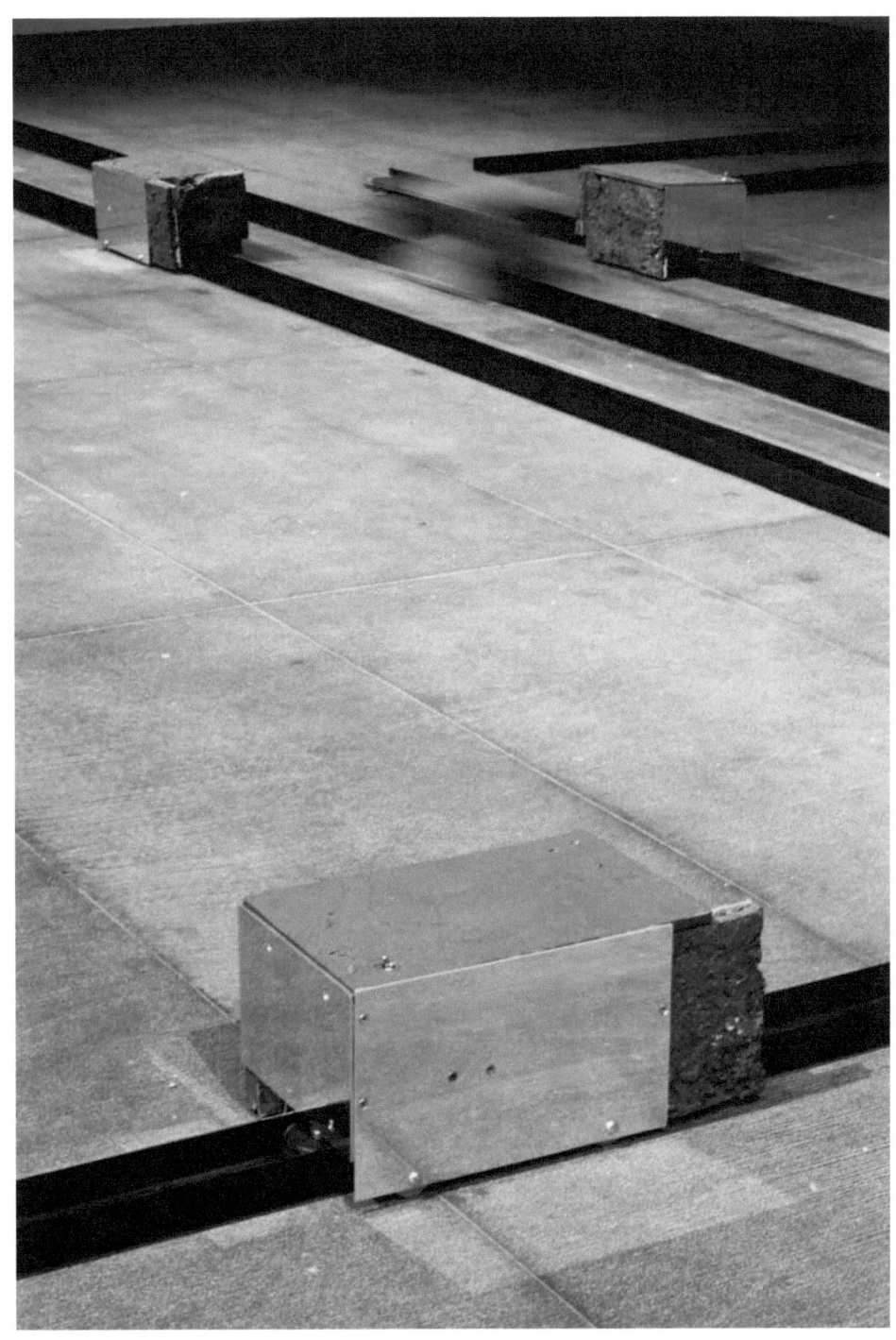

DESCRIPTION

Inside each of the piece's four moving boxes – or five sided paintings – are a battery, two motors and a set of wheels controlled by a micro-processor, which is programmed to propel the boxes forwards and backwards. The sides of the boxes are covered either in highly textured oil paint or polished aluminum. Their tops are a thin layer of paint attached to a transducer and sound module. Thus, the tops are paintings that double as speaker membranes; and, in essence, the paintings are literally moving speakers - each playing its own sound, composed by Yannick Franck.

The piece also references the musical form of a nocturne (and, equally, James McNeil Whistler's use of a limited palette of silvers, blues and greys for his similarly titled works). These formal effects have been channeled via Piet Mondrian to create an abstract choreography between the paintings, where their polished aluminum sides reflect each other in passing but never meet, echoing Franck's melancholy sounds. Machines, though – like people – are also prone to mishaps; and when the moving boxes/paintings run off course and hit the track's end, they cry out "ouch" (if they hit the forward stop) or "excuse me" (if they hit the back stop) and then return to their starting points.

The first exhibition in Taipei was kindly supported with a Senior Scholar Specialist grant from the Fulbright Program.

ACKNOWLEDGEMENTS

Chen Chang-Chih, and Rudi Punzo for video documentation.

EXHIBITION VENUES

OBORO (as part of *Dream Mechanics/Mécaniques oniriques*), Montreal, Canada, curated by Tamar Tembeck, 2016

Boston Sculptors Gallery, Boston, MA, *Mechanical Universe: Nocturne*, 2009

Kuandu Museum of Fine Arts, Taipei, Taiwan, *Collaboration: Anticipating the Art of the Future*, 2008

PRESS

KdMoFA Artist in Residence Program, p. 18. Taipei: Kuandu Museum of Fine Arts, January 2013.

McQuaid, Cate. "Various Evidence of Enigma." *The Boston Globe*, July 22, 2009.

RELATED RESIDENCY

Artist-in-Residence at the Kuandu Museum of Fine Arts, summer 2008

RELATED TALKS

National Taiwan Museum of Fine Arts, Taichung, Taiwan, 2008

Hualian Creative and Cultural Part, Hualian, Taiwan, 2008

Fulbright Center, Taipei, Taiwan, 2008

Kaoshiung Normal University, Kaoshiung, Taiwan, 2008

RELATED WORKSHOP

Collaboration: Anticipating the Art of the Future Workshop, Taipei National University of the Arts, 2008

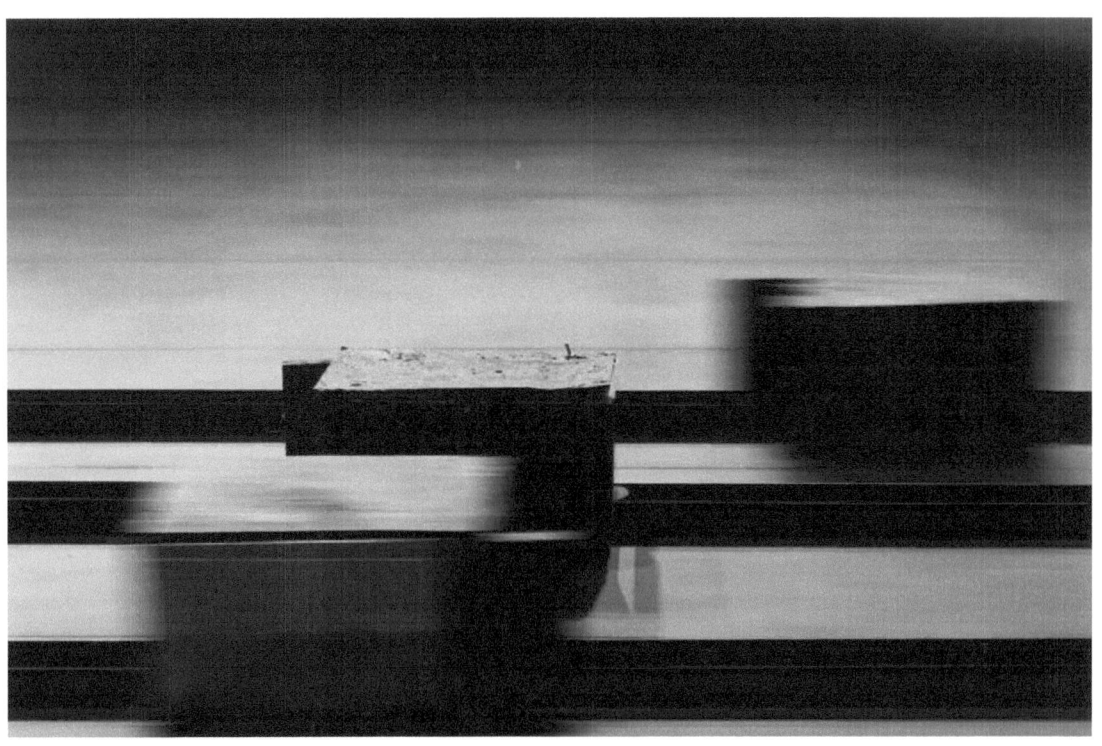

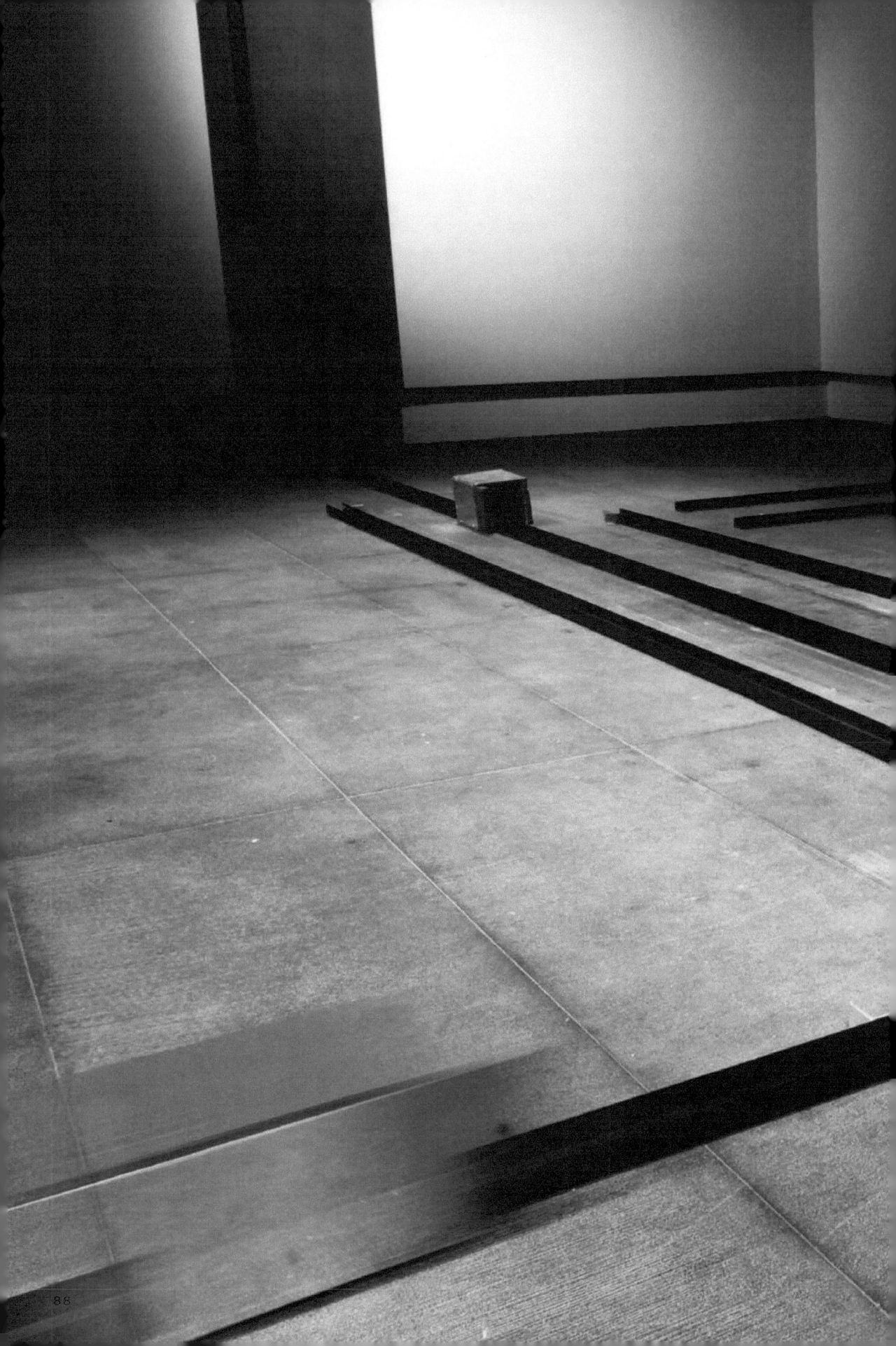

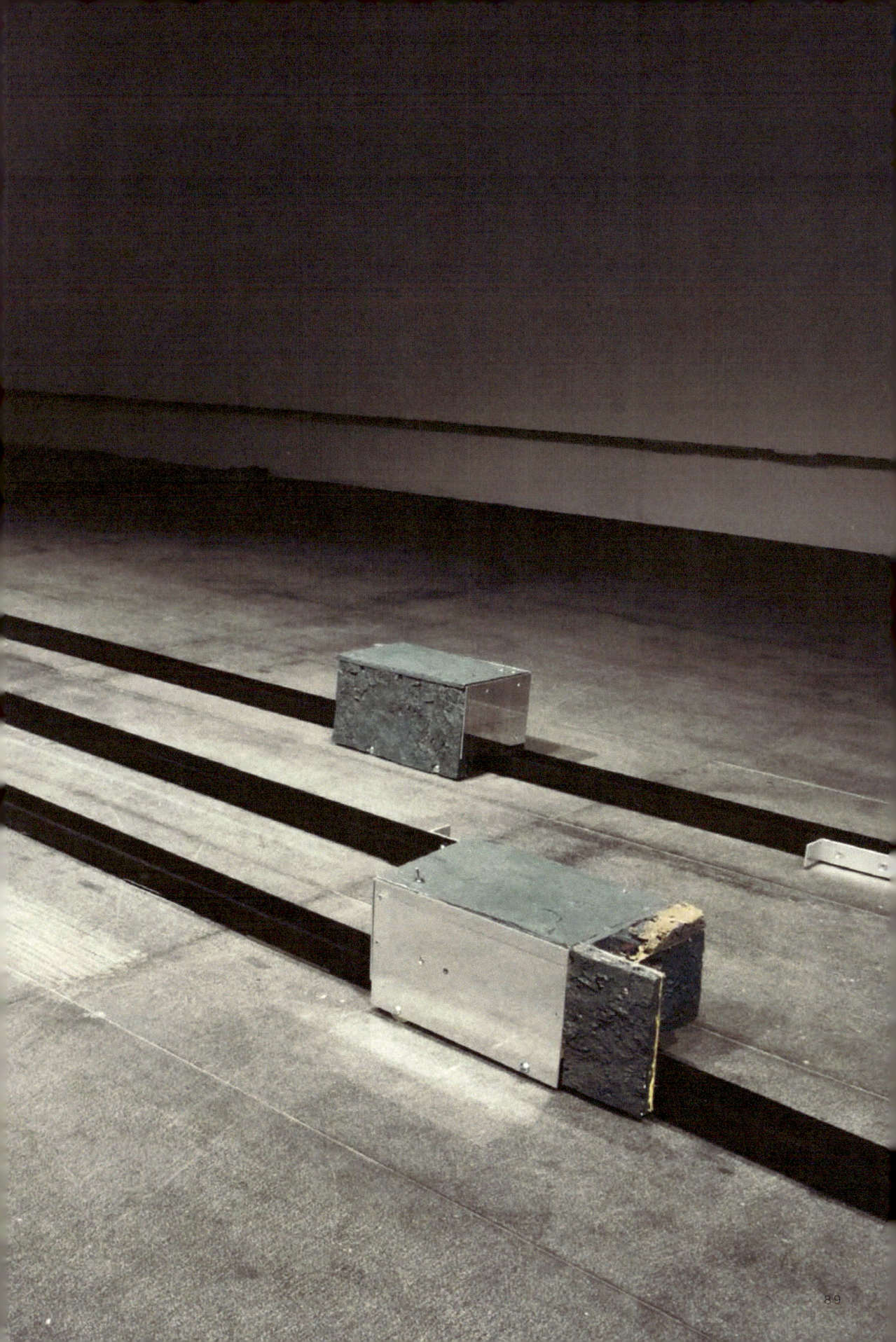

CONTEXTUALIZING

At Heart, Spike Jones

Oil and newspaper on wood, chipboard, stainless steel, aluminum, motorized/programmed "turntable," horn, speakers, sound and martini glass

Total dimensions variable; height adjustable; the three painted boxes: 13" × 6" × 5", 12" × 6" × 5", 16" × 5" × 6"; coasters: 4½" × 4½"

2002–2003/2011 (coasters and text added to the piece)

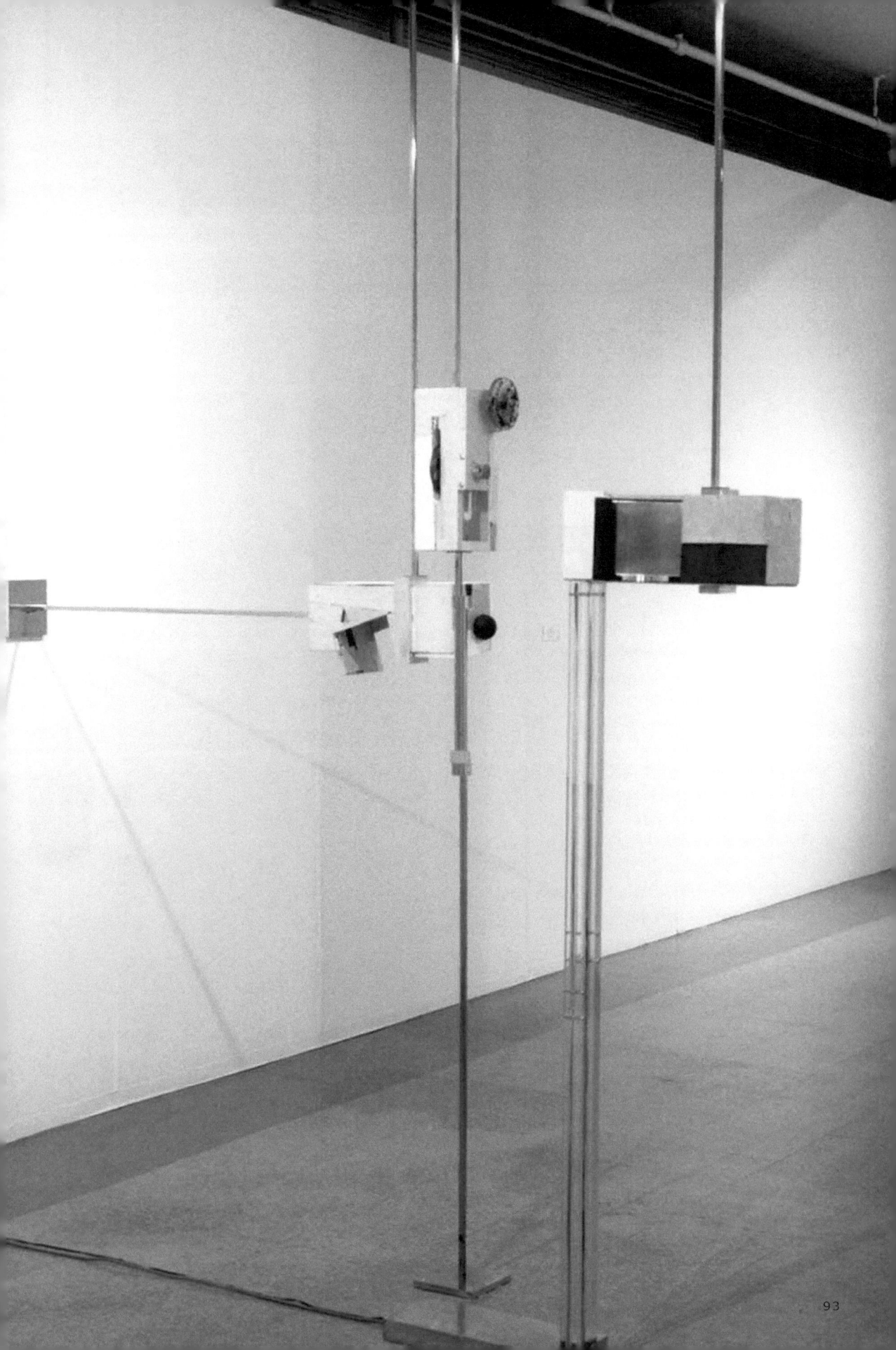

DESCRIPTION

At the touch of a button, a wackily irreverent love song (somewhat in the vein of Spike Jones' *Cocktails for Two*) starts playing through speakers mounted within one of the box-like painted and collaged constructions. A cocktail glass then spins out from another of the three painted and collaged boxes, all of which are sandwiched between the floor and ceiling by thin, square stainless steel rods. The glass dances back and forth as the song plays while lights spin around above. Meanwhile, off to one side – as explained in the accompanying wall text [1] – coasters are left on a stand for the taking. The piece is meant to be a set of quiet, elegant structures that can be arranged in various configurations. Once activated, they reveal an irreverent twist, not unlike Spike Jones' music.

ACKNOWLEDGEMENTS

Walter Lenk for programming assistance, Peter Lindenmuth for technical and mechanical assistance and Ean White for video documentation.

EXHIBITION VENUES

OBORO (as part of *Dream Mechanics/Mécaniques oniriques*), Montreal, Canada, curated by Tamar Tembeck, 2016

University of Massachusetts, Amherst, Hampden Gallery, Amherst, MA, curated by Anne LaPrade, 2011

Boston Center for the Arts, Boston, MA, *what if?*, 2003

PRESS

"Hampden Gallery, Mary Sherman." *Fine Arts Center 2010–2011*, p. 19. Amherst: UMass Amherst, 2011.

Hopkins, Randi. "Art on Its Own." *The Boston Phoenix*, October 31, 2003.

Jaeger, Luke. "Regional Reviews." *Art New England*, January/February 2004.

McQuaid, Cate. "Exhibition Encourages Artists to Alter One Another's Work." *The Boston Globe*, November 14, 2003.

REFERENCES AND NOTES

1. Take a chance: push the button.

   The romance begins: music, cocktails, a conversation starter.

   Want more? Take ONE of the little "collages" out into the world. Place it under a drink. (Instant coaster.) [2] Enjoy the aphrodisiac of being a rouge collector. The catch: Now that you've snatched the work away from those with the wherewithal to enter a gallery, it is NOT yours to keep.

   Liberate Art. Leave the work behind, give it to someone else, pass it on.

   Come on, life's short. Recycle the love. After all, isn't that what it's all about?

2. The use of the coasters was inspired by two projects organized by TransCultural Exchange. The first project was part of the 2000 London Biennale; the second entitled *The Coaster Project, Destination: The World*, took place in more than 100 sites throughout the world in 2002. For the latter, over ninety-nine artists each submitted 100 coaster-sized art works to 100 exhibition sites. Afterwards, the more than 10,000 artworks were freely distributed to the public.

   http://transculturalexchange.org/activities/the-coaster-project/

   See Appendix.

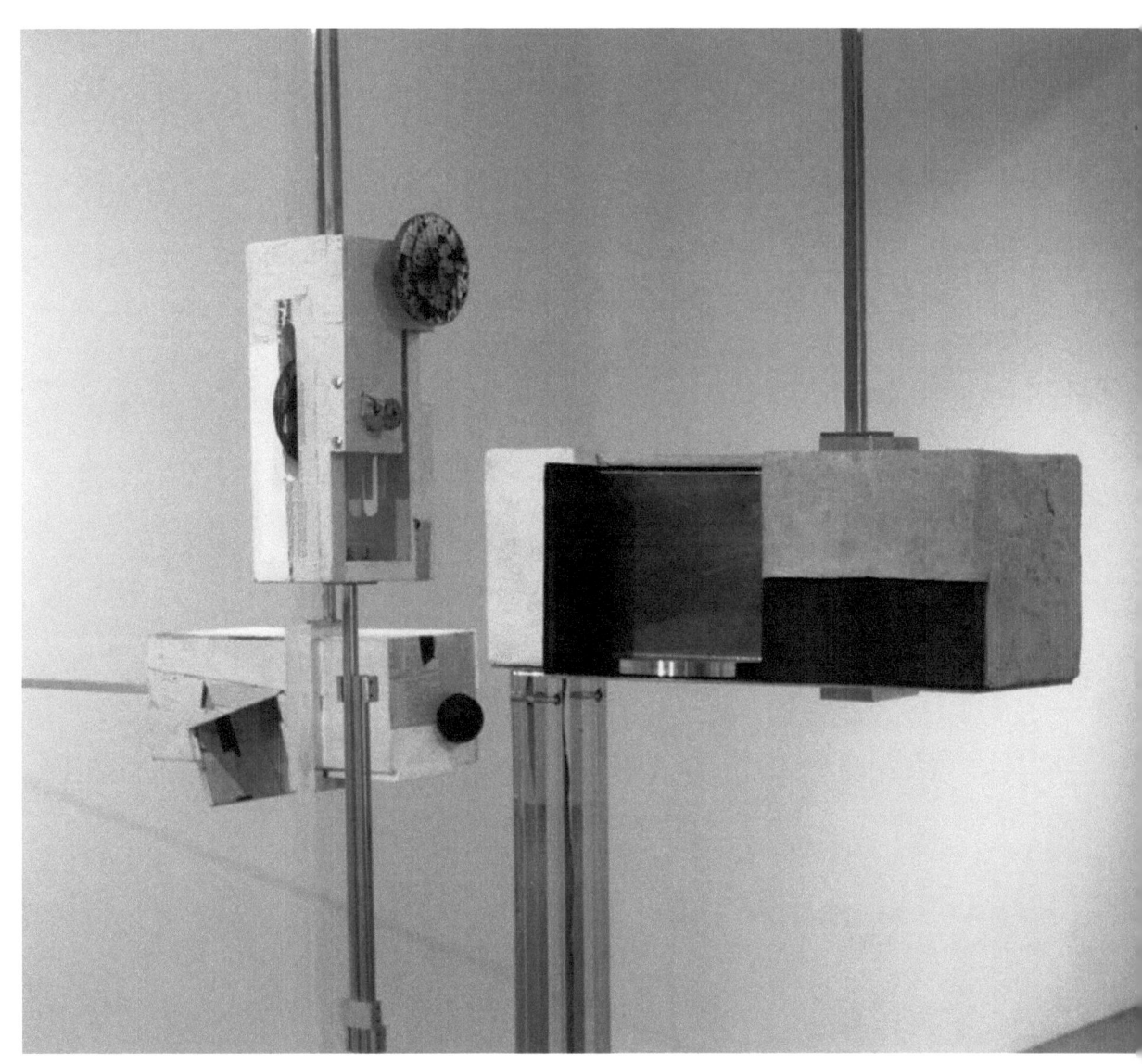

What if?

by Mary Sherman

What if a push of a button could move a painting? Or a painting was modular so you could re-arrange it? What if sculptures were on wheels so you could push them around? Or you could sit on them? Or an installation could turn your world upside down? Or disappear in minutes? What if you had the power to change an artwork to your liking?

No artwork is an island. Like everything else, an artwork is shaped not only by its creator, but by the context and surroundings in which it finds itself. A painting by van Gogh inevitably looks different in a modernist, clean white space than in its originally-intended turn-of-the-century Parisian apartment with colored walls and overstuffed furniture.

Likewise, a Duchamp shovel changes meaning dramatically when viewed in a museum or a hardware store. This, in part, was Duchamp's point. But what is often overlooked – or at least downplayed – is the impact that someone else (such as the owner of an artwork) or some other place (such as a contemporary home or gallery setting) might have on a work of art. *what if?* examines this subtle, but crucial element of the artistic practice.

At the dawn of the 21st century, it no longer seems possible for artists to think of themselves as the sole creators of their work's aesthetic impact. It just isn't so. Once out of their hands, like every other creation, art takes on a life of its own. Pieces age, are conserved, move from place to place and are adapted to new sets of circumstances.

This became blatantly apparent to me during a project that I worked on with the international artists' collaborative TransCultural Exchange. For *The Coaster Project, Destination: The World*, over 100 artists made 100 individual art works in the guise of coasters. These then were re-packaged and sent back to the artists, so that each of the participating artists received a set of every other artist's works, displayed them in their home own and, afterwards, gave them away to the public for free.

Something else also occurred that made me realize how much context also can influence a viewer's appreciation and understanding of a work of art: initially, as the artworks arrived at the offices of TransCultural Exchange, I was surprised to find that all the pieces seemed vaguely "international." By this I mean that in only the rarest instances would anyone be able to name the country from where the works were sent, but when the press coverage and images of the exhibitions started coming into the office, it was very easy to guess where the exhibitions and installations had taken place. The shows of the composite sets of works looked different in Finland than in China; different in India than Germany or Switzerland, etc. Part of this had to do with the features and dress of the visitors to the exhibits, and part of it had to do with the surrounding architecture, but part of it also had to do with the way in which the local artists had installed the exhibits.

Some of the works also took on different meanings in different locations. One of the artists, Vince Garguilo, for instance, produced plaster casts of hands of people at New York's Parsons School of Art and Design. All of these were numbered, placed in a box and shipped to one of the world sites. Coincidentally, it turned out that the site in China received cast, number 64, the handprint of Gargiulo's student Leah Gadd. In China many visitors saw the hand emerging from the white disc as a commentary on the Tiananmen Square incident, which took place on June (the sixth month) 4th, or 64 – a perfectly logical, albeit erroneous, interpretation.

The idea that art works can mean different things to different people is not new – nor is the idea that a location can impact a work. However, most artists continue to hold onto the modernist notion that an artwork is the creation of a sole, individual creator and thus has an inherent fixed quality that is absolutely unshakeable. This show hopes to re-examine that notion and to offer a more embracing view of art; one that recognizes the artist's "handprint" in their artwork, while also realizing that the experience and contemplation of an art object is not limited to the boundaries of a painting's frame or a sculpture's planes.

The exhibit *what if?* [2] includes the work of five artists [3] who acknowledge, relish and accept the impact of the audience, collector or other artist as well as the physical, historical and cultural context of an exhibition site. These artists are submitting pieces (installations, videos, glass paintings and sculptures) that their exhibiting colleagues will change during the fourth week – vis-à-vis the works' context. The public also will be invited to submit ideas for how they would imagine the work if they owned it. The artists then, on November 17th, will change their work again, according to the selected viewers' suggestions.

The aim of the show is to illuminate the artist's role as a creative instigator. By extension, it will invite the public to consider and participate in the artistic creation – which they inevitably will do when they purchase or are given an art work and turn it into part of their own creation as a component of their home or art collection. Ultimately, the various mutations of each artist's work might lead the original creators to consider new, provocative and fruitful avenues to explore in their future work.

Stay tuned.

REFERENCES AND NOTES

1. More information on this project is available at www.transculturalexhange.org/coasterproject.

2. Mary Sherman, *what if?*, Mills Gallery, Boston, 2003, press release:

    What if a push of a button could move a painting? Or a painting was modular so you could re-arrange it? What if sculptures were on wheels so you could push them around? Or you could sit on them? Or an installation could turn your world upside down? Or disappear in minutes? What if you had the power to change an art work to your liking?

    When the Mills Gallery re-opens on October 29, the artists of *What If?* will have done just that. On October 27, they are meeting to re-arrange, add to and change their fellow exhibitors' works. (The public will have a chance to do the same by dropping suggestions for altering the works into a box at the gallery. Then, on November 7, the artists will re-create their works according to selected audience members' proposed suggestions.)

3. Kelly Kaczynski, Peter Lindenmuth, Urban Ramstedt, Larimer Richards, Mary Sherman, James Tellin and, in the Project Space, images from *The Coaster Project, Destination: The World* and the MIT student collaborative team of Brian Hoying, Youri Legrand and Alessandra Sabelli.

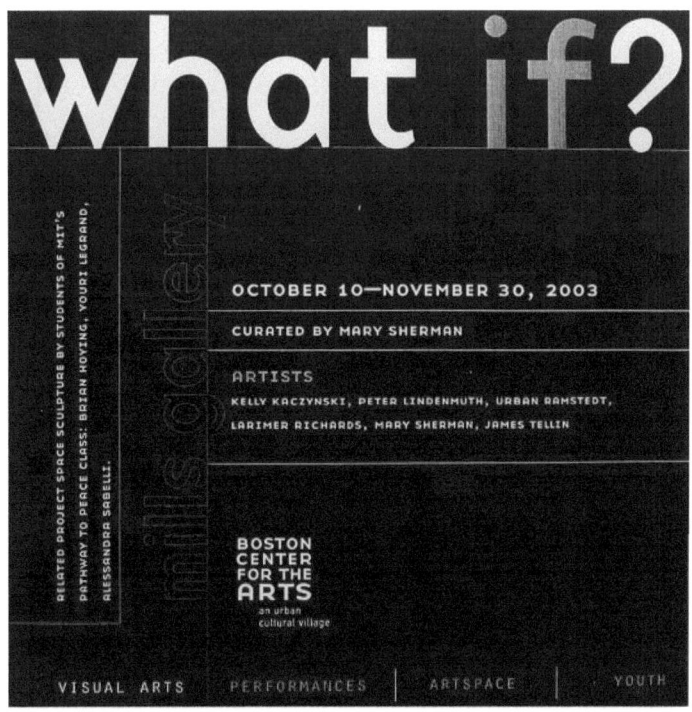

Invitation card for *what if?* at the Mills Gallery, Boston, 2003.

The Coaster Project: The 2000 London Biennale

Inkjet Print

4" × 4"

Edition: 50

2000

2000 London Biennial Art Exhibition Transcultural Exchange

May 29, under your drink, at Cynthia's Cyberbar 4 Tooley St

'in London for the 2000 London Biennial.
Everything arrived OK
'would love it if you could join us at the exhibition on Monday, May 29, at Cynthia's Cyberbar, where the art can be found under your drink.
'a perfect excuse for a toast!
The artist-collaborative Transcultural Exchange (Mary Sherman, Malvina Sammarone, Sunghoon Yang, Victoria Hanks, Bill Rock, Heejung Kim, Theodore Cantrell), participants in the 2000 London Biennial.

www.cynbbar.co.uk under the London Bridge

Transcultural Exchange Art Exhibition

DESCRIPTION

In 2000, the artist collective TransCultural Exchange (consisting, for this project, of Mary Sherman, Malvina Sammarone, Sunghoon Yang, Victoria Hanks, Bill Rock, Heejung Kim and Theodore Cantrell) produced its fifth international venture *The Coaster Project* for the London Biennale, which was founded and directed by David Medalla. Their project took place at Cynthia's Bridge Bar & Lounge in London. For their participation – instead of showing their artworks on the walls in a typical exhibition fashion and in the spirit of that Biennale's free-for-all premise – each participating artist made 50 unique, 4" x 4" artworks that were exhibited and given away for free under the patrons' drinks in the guise of coasters. 50 of these were the limited edition black and white invitation.

EXHIBITION VENUE

Cynthia's Bridge Bar & Lounge, London, England, *The Coaster Project*, 2000

House of Cards

Collage on chipboard

Dimensions variable; 50 pieces: 4" × 4"

2000

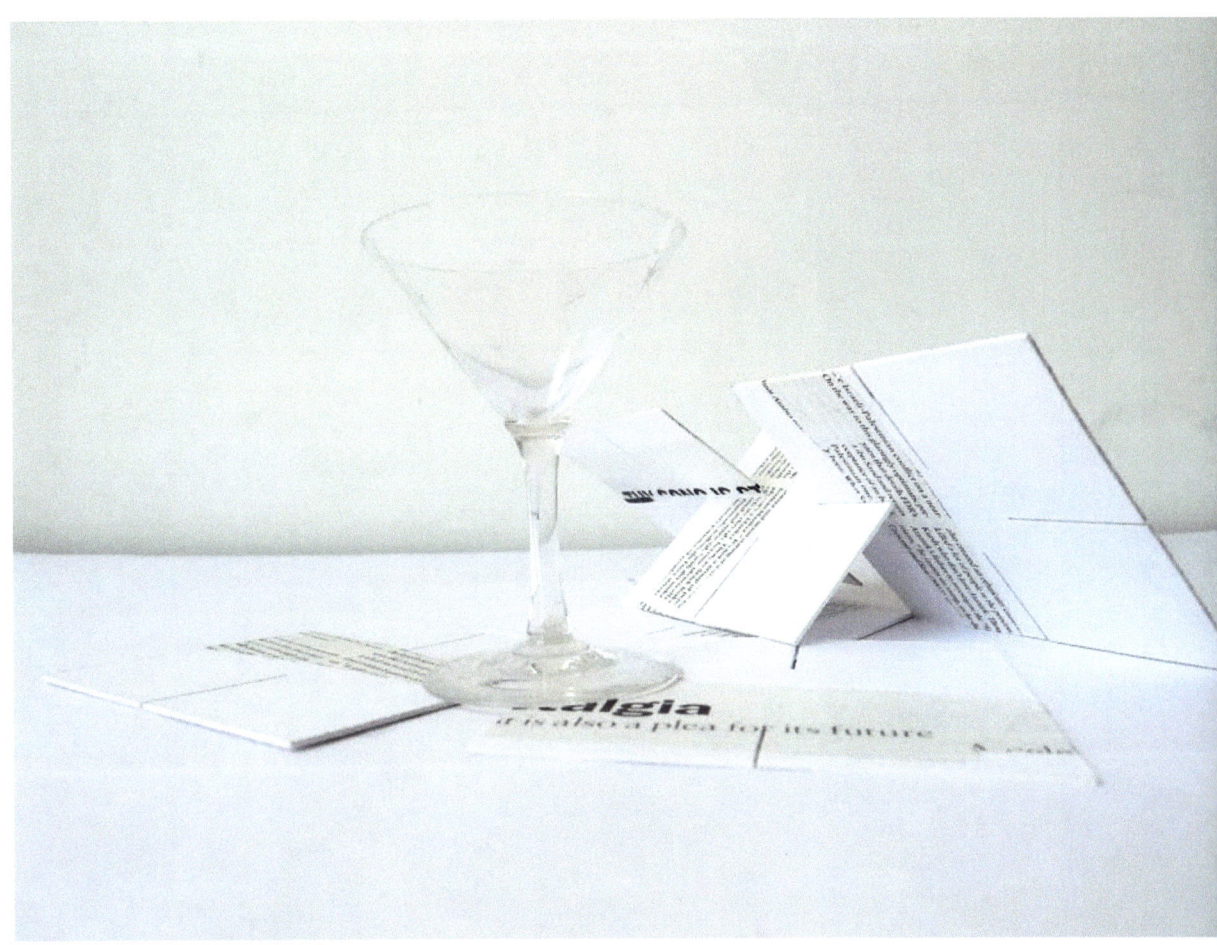

DESCRIPTION

This work was made for the artist collective TransCultural Exchange's participation in the 2000 London Biennale, which took place at Cynthia's Bridge Bar & Lounge. Each piece was meant to double as a coaster and collage and notched so that if a person collected a number of them, they could build them into sculptures. As was later the case with the coasters made for *The Coaster Project, Destination: The World* [1] and *At Heart, Spike Jones*, the artworks were not for sale; instead, they were left under the patrons' drinks, free for the taking.

EXHIBITION VENUE

Cynthia's Bridge Bar & Lounge, London, England, *The Coaster Project*, 2000

REFERENCES AND NOTES

1. See Appendix.

MECHANIZING

Le Matin de la Nuit/Ballet Mécanique

Oil paint on wood, hand-made timer, motor, aluminum, music box, buzzer, light and plexi-glass

168" (adjustable) × 144" × 60"

Video documentation: https://vimeo.com/123823668 [1]

2008

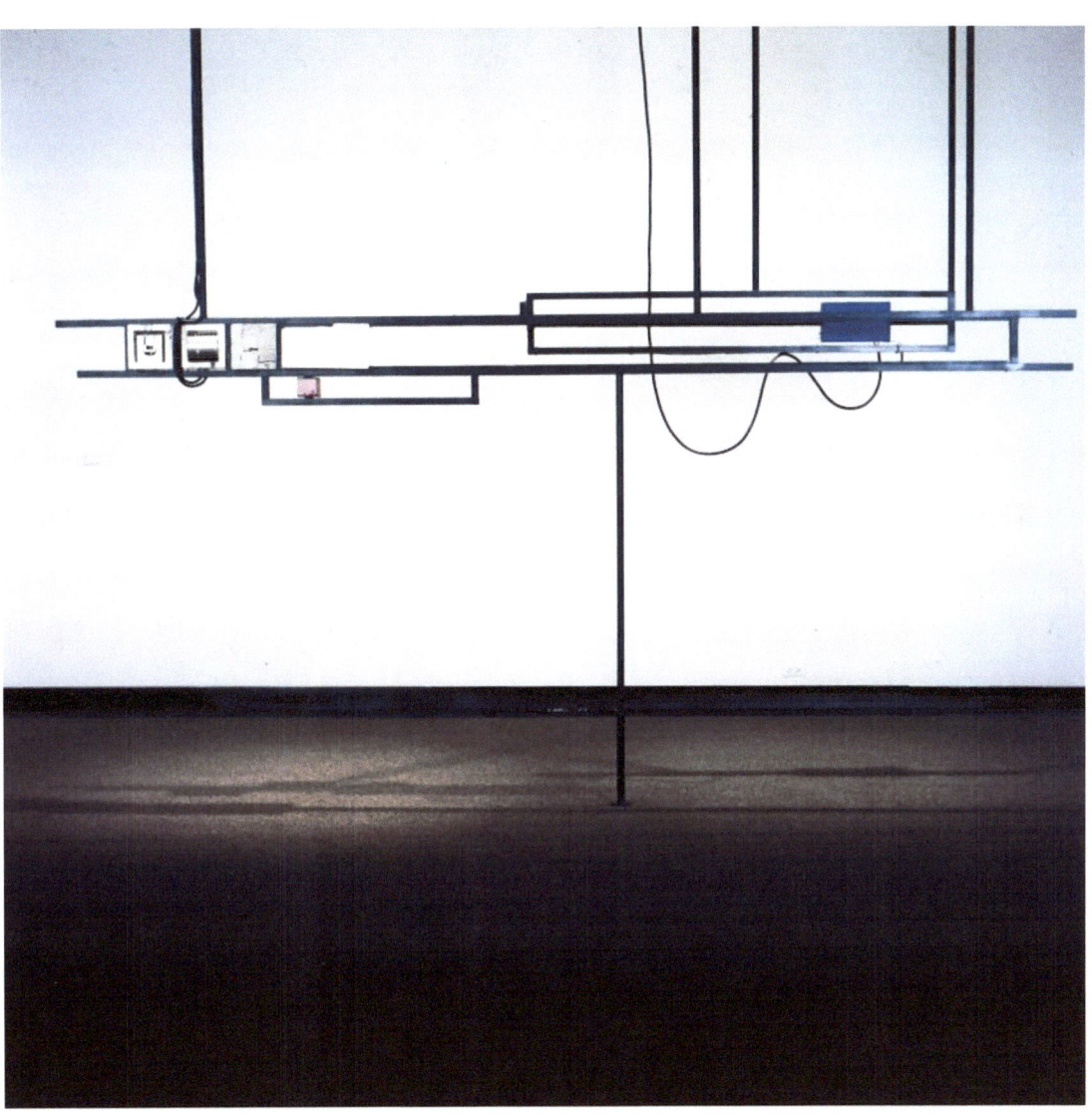

DESCRIPTION

Inspired by Georges Antheil's *Ballet Mécanique*, *Le Matin de la Nuit/Ballet Mécanique* consists of five discrete paintings mounted within two hanging, linear frames. When the audience enters, a motion sensor activates the work's timer, which is programmed to set off the other elements so that they 'perform' at different sequenced times. First is a stepper motor, which bangs against its wooden frame. After it has finished its performance, the larger white box slowly winds its way back and forth along one of the aluminum frameworks, tripping off the blue music box behind it, followed by the sound of a door buzzer and ending with the illumination of the red, plexi-glass box. Together, the movements, sounds and visuals are to rhythmically and metaphorically suggest the cacophony of life's daily grind.

ACKNOWLEDGEMENTS

Peter Lindenmuth and his associate William Stephens for technical and mechanical assistance and George Bossarte for the circuitry.

EXHIBITION VENUES

OBORO (as part of *Dream Mechanics/Mécaniques oniriques*), Montreal, Canada, curated by Tamar Tembeck, 2016

The Fuller Museum of Art, *TransCultural Exchange*, Brockton, MA, curated by Denise Markonish, 2002

REFERENCES AND NOTES

1. The music in the video is the "soundtrack" for the video. It is not a part of the artwork itself. The buzzer, the sounds generated by the blue "music box", and the motors' banging and grinding, however, are integral to the piece.

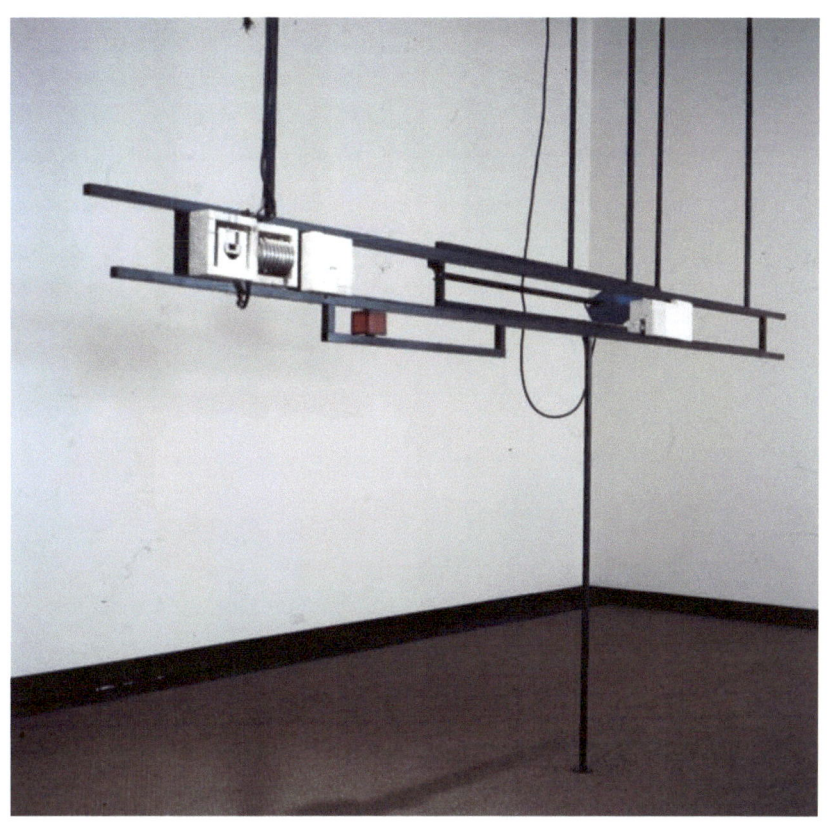
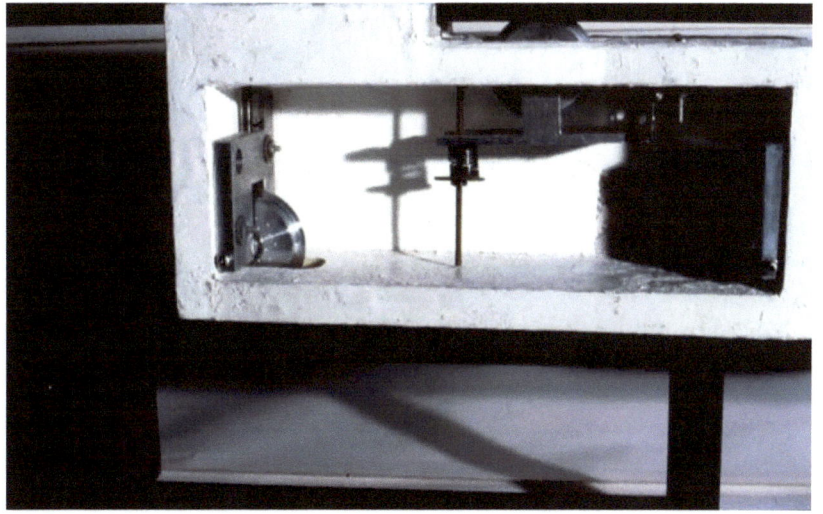

An Urban Sky

Oil paint on wood, newspaper, motor, steel, aluminum couplings, and/or paper maché tree and/or sound

Total dimensions variable; each panel: 14" × 14" × 2"

Video documentation: https://vimeo.com/125021973 [1]

1999/2001 (sound added)

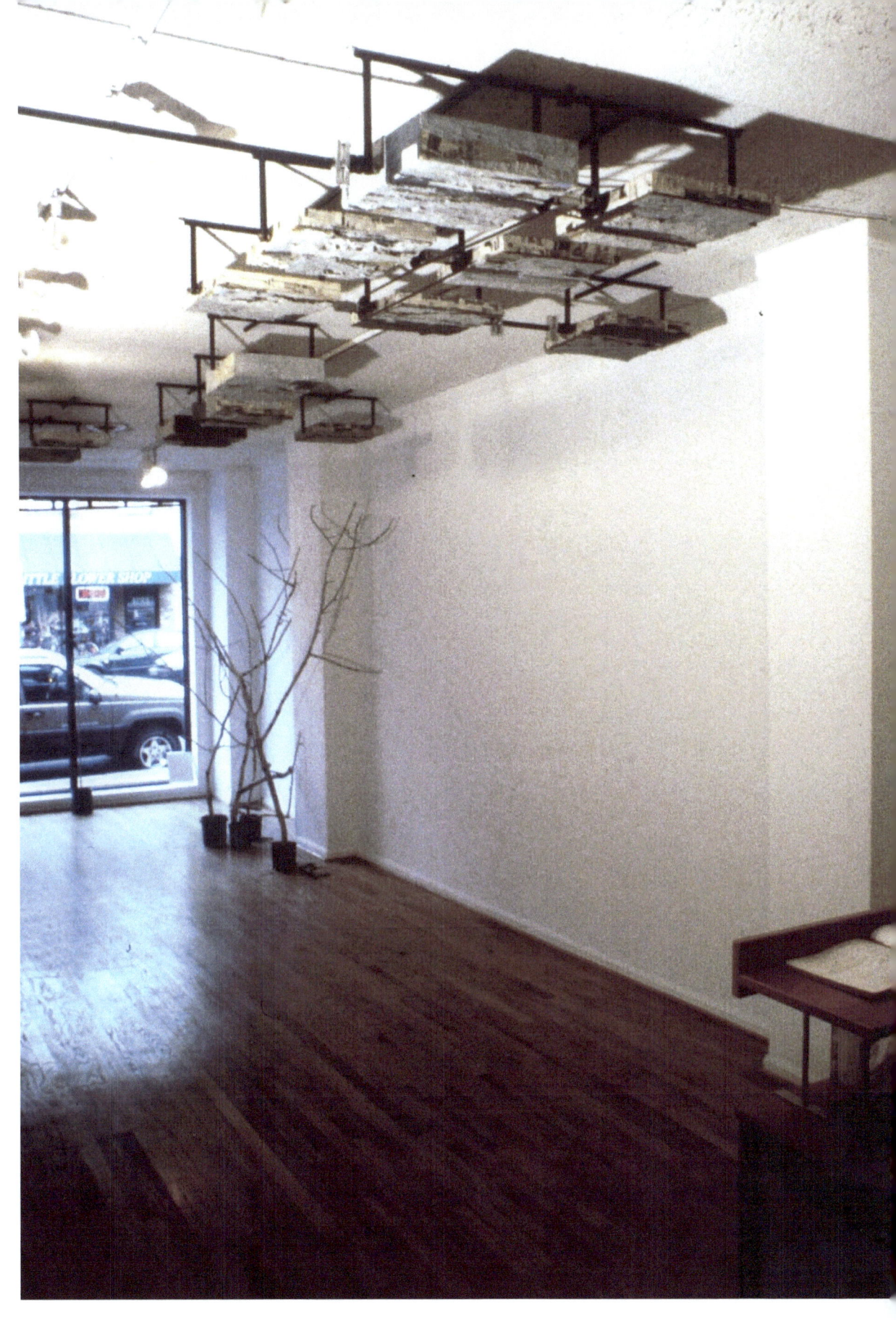

DESCRIPTION

An Urban Sky was conceived to be an updated, modular version of a Baroque ceiling painting, made for city dwellers with little access to the sky. It is highly adaptable to different settings and meant to be so. The piece consists of sixteen painted panels, nine of which are motorized. They can either be wall-mounted (to suggest looking out at the sky along the horizon) or ceiling-mounted (as in a traditional Baroque ceiling painting). One side of each is highly textured and painted cool grey; the other is midnight blue enamel. A motor flips the panels over to suggest a change from day to night. A button (floor pedal) is also included, recreating the sound of rain and thunder at the drop of a foot; and the piece can be presented with two background options: the color of the wall or ceiling on which it is displayed or a backdrop of black panels.

ACKNOWLEDGEMENTS

Peter Lindenmuth for technical and mechanical assistance.

EXHIBITION VENUES

Cushing-Martin Gallery at Stonehill College, Easton, MA, *Move Me: Kineticism in Art*, 2008

Art Complex Museum, Duxbury, MA, Gadgets, *Gizmos and Games* (catalog), 2002

University of Massachusetts, Hampden Gallery, Amherst, MA, *New England/New York/New Talent*, curated by Jeannette Ingherman, 2001

The Dietrich Gallery, Allston, MA, *The Dietrich Biennial*, 2001

Trans Hudson Gallery, NY, NY, *TransCultural Exchange: nomads forever*, 2000

Boston College, McMullen Museum of Art, Chestnut Hill, MA, *25 Years of Excellence*, 1999

District Fine Arts, Washington, DC, *Mary Sherman: An Urban Sky*, 1999

PRESS

Barber, Christina L. "Up Next." *The Daily Hampshire Gazette*, March 13, 2001.

Giuliano, Charles. "Boston College: Celebrating 25 Years of Excellence in the Visual Arts." *Boston.sidewalk.com*, August 8, 1999.

Knox, Robert. "Collection of Contraptions: New Art Installation Offers Fanciful Look at Gadgets." *The Boston Globe*, September 19, 2002.

Temin, Christine. "Boston College Show Showcases Faculty." *The Boston Globe*, July 30, 1999.

REFERENCES AND NOTES

1. The music in the video for *An Urban Sky* is the "soundtrack" for the video. It is not part of *An Urban Sky*. *An Urban Sky* is silent except for the sound of the panels turning and the rain and thunder, which are activated by stepping on a red, floor-mounted button.

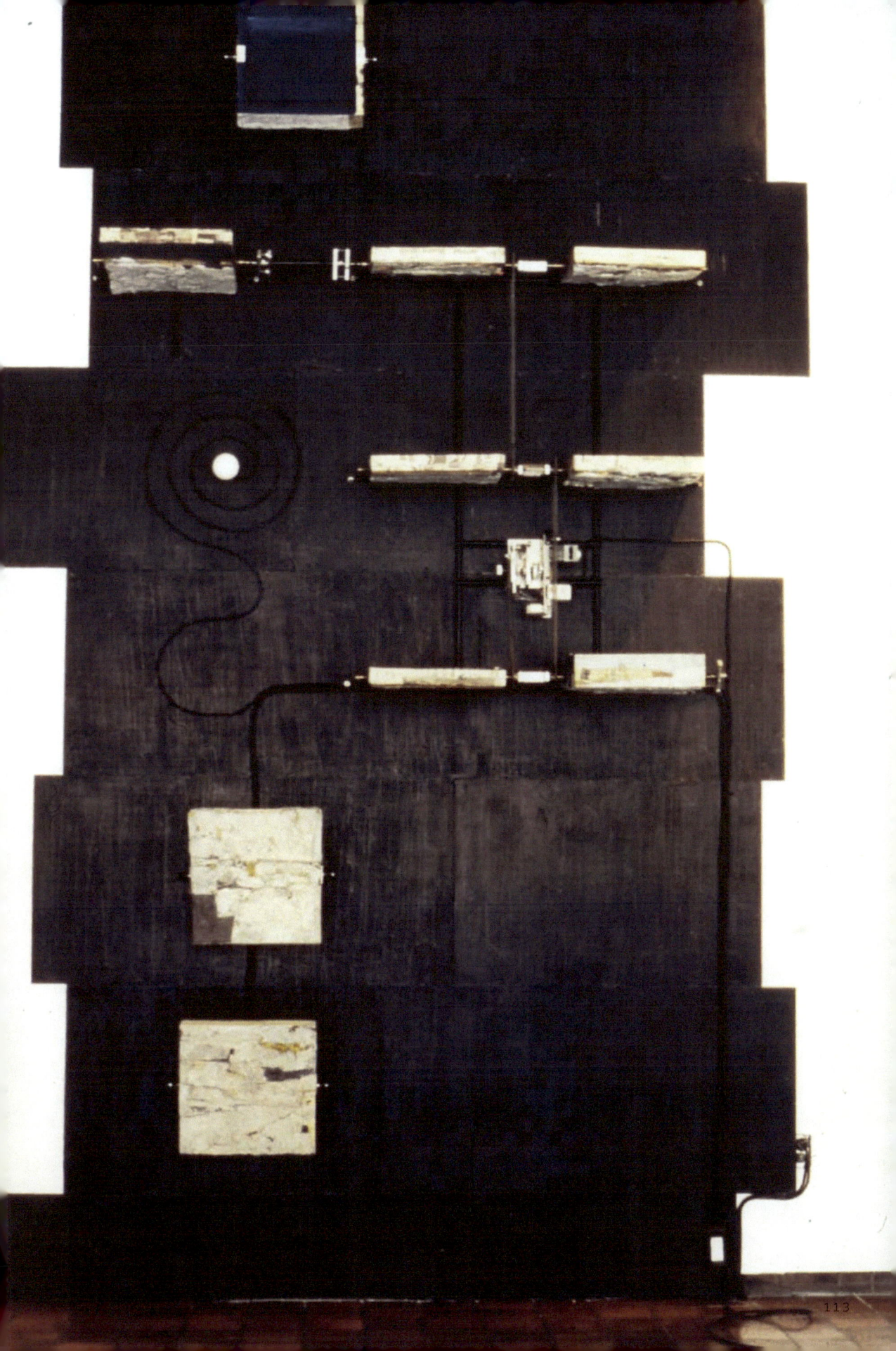

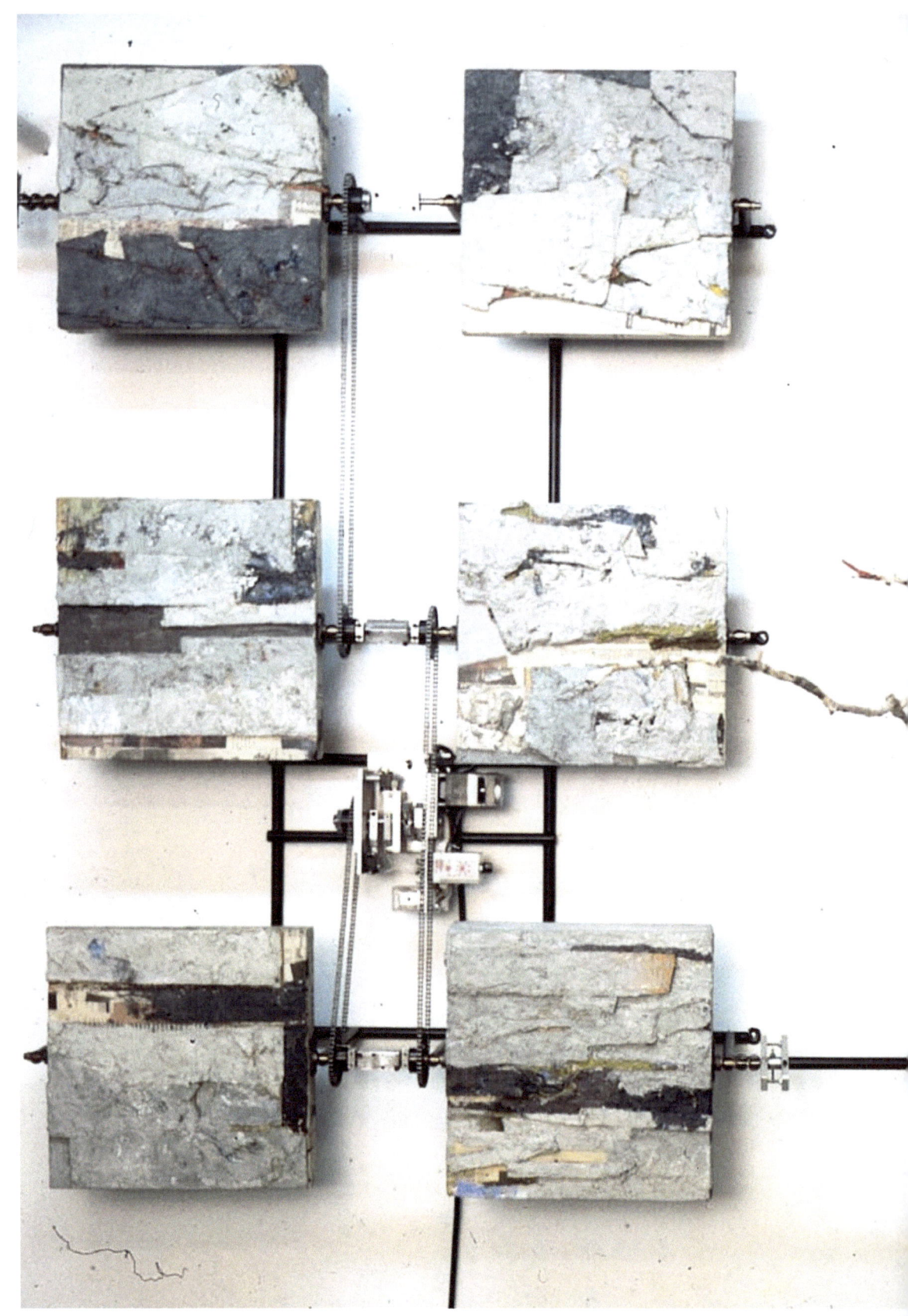

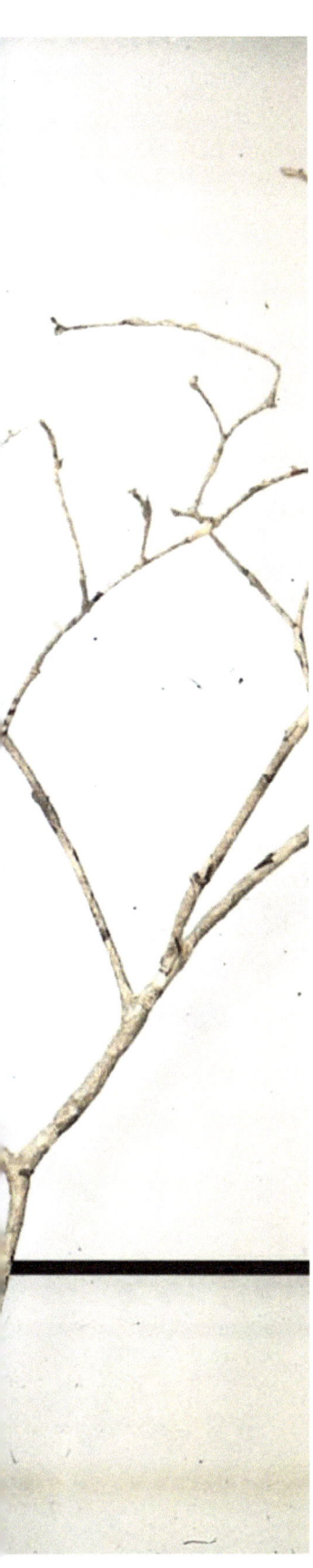

An Urban Sky Miniature

Oil paint, newspaper, motor, steel, aluminum couplings and optional paper maché trees

8" × 30" × 4"; each panel: 1" × 1" × ¼"

2001

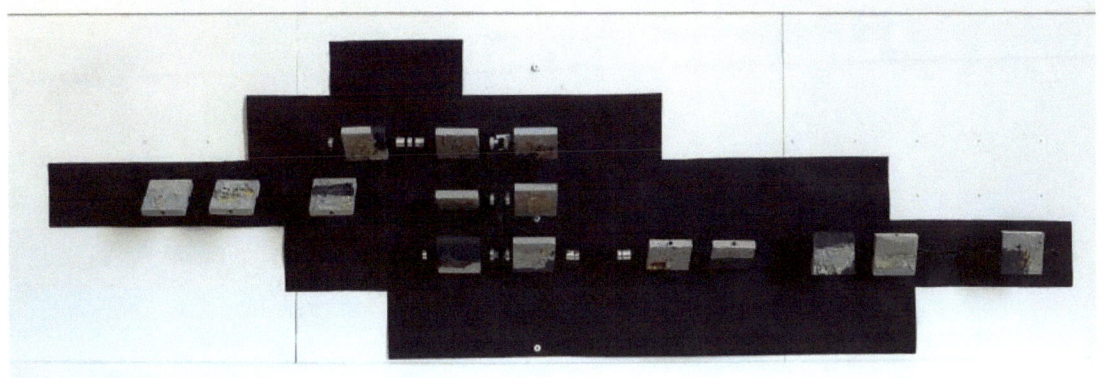

DESCRIPTION

An Urban Sky Miniature was conceived as a Fabergé like folly – a miniature, fanciful world. It is a replica of – not the model for – *An Urban Sky*; and, as in *An Urban Sky*, nine of the sixteen individual panels are motorized. One side of the panels is highly textured and painted cool grey; another is midnight blue. A motor flips the panels over to suggest a changing skyline. Also, like those in the larger version, the individual panels can be re-configured.

ACKNOWLEDGEMENTS

Peter Lindenmuth for technical and mechanical assistance.

EXHIBITION VENUES

Casa Italiana Zerilli-Marimo, NY, NY, *Venice*, 2001

Arlington Arts Center, Arlington, MA, *Constructions* (miniature version), 2001

PRESS

"Arts in Brief." *The Boston Herald*, January 18, 2001.

"*Constructions*." The Boston Globe, August 19, 2001.

Muther, Christopher. "Quick Hits: Art." *The Boston Globe*, August 23, 2001.

O'Neal, Lauren. "Center for the Arts Exhibit Explores Real and Imagined *Constructions*." *The Arlington Advocate*, September 20, 2001.

Unger, Miles. "Spotlight Art: Constructions." *Boston Magazine*, August 2001.

TALKING

Interview

by Lanfrano Aceti
with Mary Sherman

LANFRANCO ACETI: *Your practice is so varied – you have a studio practice, curate, run a non-profit organization, write and teach. How do you account for all this? Do you find this confuses people?*

MARY SHERMAN: Well, someone once called me a pixie. Maybe it's true. Pixies are known to do the unexpected.

But, yes, it is problematic. People prefer to know who and what they are dealing with; and if you can't give them a simple, all encompassing answer, they grow uncomfortable. It's not surprising. It's disruptive to run up against someone or something that isn't easy to place. It means you have to make room for something new – even if that room is only mental. And life is hard enough without loading more things onto it.

Yet I believe that artists have a responsibility to pique this discomfort. And one of the beauties about art is that people expect the unexpected of it. Art is where people go to be transported out of their lives; to be surprised, tickled, provoked, inspired. . . so I believe we owe them this.

And, I take this responsibility seriously. For instance, part of what I wanted to do with *Waiting for Yves* was to challenge the expectation that an exhibit is an indoor space with works arranged around a room. So, for that piece, I "wallpapered" a room with blue marks so people would feel like they walked into a sky (although some people felt it was an ocean, which I also liked). Only later did the reference to Yves Klein's *Le Vide* [(*The Specialization of Sensibility in the Raw Material State into Stabilized Pictorial Sensibility, The Void*)] dawn on me. How I didn't make that connection from the start I'll never know! But, of course, even our own thoughts are capable of surprising us. And, for me this was a very welcomed treat.

This is also very much the way I usually work. I start out with an idea for another way of considering something – usually something to do with painting (since I'm so obsessed with that medium) – and then other things come into play. Some turn into dead ends; some into unimagined delights. For me, the process is very, very slow and rarely easy. I mean it took me decades to figure out how to hear a painting. And I'm still no closer to understanding what defines it. But what can one do but try? Or to quote [Samuel] Beckett, "Ever tried. Ever failed. No matter. Try Again. Fail again. Fail better."

Well, let's talk about this a bit more. You consider yourself a painter, right?

Yes. Although I know I'm probably the only person who would call me that. But it all depends on one's definition of painting, I suppose. And this is something, as I've said, that I've been trying to figure out for decades.

I began with a fairly academic training, only to slowly become much more interested in the physicality of paint itself (versus its ability to create credible illusions of three-dimensionality). This led me to treat oil paint almost like it was clay. By that time, the paintings had grown so heavy that they could stand on their own. And then one day I came into the studio and thought, "Why not just leave them there on the floor? Who said a painting has to be on a wall?"

For one exhibit, then, I put nails on two opposing walls and hung some on one wall, some on the other and left some lying and standing on the floor. I thought of the whole room as a painting, and every so often I'd go in and change its composition. For another piece *Bolts of Blue*, I stretched a painting between two walls, thinking, "Who said a painting has to just sit on one?"

Then one day I got stuck. I wanted to make an updated version of a Baroque ceiling painting – what would become *An Urban Sky*. So I painted all these panels on the front and back with the idea that the panels would flip over to suggest night changing to day. It never occurred to me while making all these that I'd need a motor and a certain amount of engineering know-how to make this happen. But, at that point, I really didn't even know what a gear head or servomotor was, let alone much about the difference between AC and DC power.

I was made really miserable by this realization, but then someone told me about this retired engineer Peter Lindenmuth who sometimes works with artists. I immediately called him up and he offered to help. To keep the costs down, he agreed to work out the gearing and mechanisms; and I agreed to appear at the drop of a phone call to machine the parts, even though I had never done anything like this before.

Complicating the situation was Peter's thought that I could also use the time to learn how to machine; and so every part was custom made. Thus in less than three months, Peter taught me the basics of how to machine aluminum and weld. And even when I welded the piece to the metal table and later nearly caught the workbench on fire, Peter unflinchingly continued to tell me I was doing fine. But, like everything there, nothing was as straightforward as it sounded. The strap on the welding goggles had long ago worn out, so I had to partially hold them on and weld at the same time. Not only that, but they were so old that it was difficult to see out of them. Thus, to check my work, Peter and I would have to synchronize turning off the welding torch so that we could safely remove our goggles to gauge my progress. On another day I was looking all around for the table saw: It took moving about ten boxes to find it. Then, near the end, once we had the piece assembled and the panels rotating, I panicked: the piece looked too big to fit in my car. Peter was unfazed. "We can just cut off the back of your car," he suggested, assuring me that it could be welded back on. Luckily the piece fit into the car with absolutely no room to spare.

Peter and his machine shop were really a new world for me – and a fantastic one at that; a place where anything and everything seemed possible. Although it may have taken us a while to locate the screwdrivers, the metal lathe and milling machines were always in top form. Opera was broadcast on Sundays (at full blast). And every evening at seven, work stopped so that Peter could make dinner for whoever was still there. I'll never forget one day saying I couldn't stay for dinner and, all day long, them encouraging me to stay. Finally I testily asked, "What's so special about tonight that I must be here for dinner?" Turns out it was martini night.

I could go on and on, but suffice it to say that Peter and his machine shop, Nexus (and later his friends George Bossarte and Walter Lenk, who taught me to program) changed my life. Any idea I had, they helped me do it. One day, for instance, I asked if we could make a painting go across the room (for *Le Matin de La Nuit/Ballet Mécanique*). And, after a short pause, Peter exclaimed, "Cool! Let's get George." Meaning, the answer was yes.

And how did TransCultural Exchange come into all of this?

Well, one could say that TransCultural Exchange shares my doubts about how the world operates. In the '80s – long before I encountered Nexus – artists pretty much showed in galleries. In fact, the art world was booming then. For the most part, gallerists handled artists' careers (or else you hung your work up in a coffee shop, sent slides out for competitions – things like that – and hoped for the best).

People forgot that things hadn't always been that way, that Warhol fronted a number of projects, Rauschenberg produced *9 Evenings: Theatre & Engineering*. . . but two decades later, the commercial system was on the upswing.

At that time, I was living in Chicago and also had just started showing in my first gallery and writing art criticism for the *Chicago Sun-Times*. That is also when I met these two Viennese architects – Christina Prantl and Alexander Runser – from my days as a student abroad in Vienna. They had the idea to help their artist friends stage an exchange exhibit. So, they asked if I would be interested, and I told them I was absolutely interested, as were a group of my friends. And so we got permission to use the abandoned, soon-to-be-condos Ludwig Drum factory for the show and came up with the name of TransCultural Exchange for ourselves. Then we had the good fortune of Ed Paschke loaning us a piece for the exhibit and Wim Wenders giving us permission to reprint one of his essays in *Another Chicago Magazine*, which had agreed to have their next edition act as the show's catalog. We then staged an auction and dance to raise the money for shipping, asked Facets Multimedia Centre to host an accompanying film series and, not long afterwards, had about a dozen Viennese artists on our hands installing their works. And from there, we took all the works to Vienna to show at WUK Kunsthalle. It was a lot like the kinds of projects and conferences you do. An opportunity arises or you have an idea and you just make it happen. That's what we did. I mean, why not? It took a lot of work. It was a lot of headaches to be sure, but I'm very proud of what we accomplished.

So TransCultural Exchange started in Chicago, not Boston?

Yes, not long after the Chicago/Vienna exchange, I left Chicago; and the artists there pretty much disbanded. I then had a hard time drumming up any interest in TransCultural Exchange in Boston. So nothing happened for a while. Then, when I was in graduate school in New York, I got to know a gallery owner in Chelsea named Joseph Szoecs, and one day he asked a friend and me if we wanted to use his gallery [Trans Hudson] for a show that August. Of course, we said yes! I missed the camaraderie of TransCultural Exchange and of making something – like a painting – out of nothing. So TransCultural Exchange was revived. The show was *no boundaries* and it consisted of my work and and the work of some of my fellow graduate students who also were exploring this notion of working between disciplines. After that, one of the other artists, Sunghoon Yang, arranged a show for us in Seoul, and then we were back again in New York and it just kept growing.

So you were now curating?

Well, I'm not sure it could be called curating – because I was also exhibiting, which is much more commonplace now; but, then, it was not so usual. And to do so on an international level was even rarer.

At what point, then, did TransCultural Exchange start working with an even more globally diverse group of artists? The Coaster Project, Destination the World took place on seven continents, right?

Yes, that's right. It all started with my seeing an ad in *Flash Art* for the artist David Medalla's London Biennale. The ad said that to participate, you had to submit a picture of yourself with an arrow in front of Piccadilly Circus, and then find a place for your exhibit. That seemed doable. (This was the early days of Photoshop, so we photoshopped ourselves into Piccadilly Circus, submitted the application and were in.)

Then we needed a place to show. One of the other artists, Vicki Hanks, thought we should be able to easily get a bar to let us have a show and – since our shows were not the normal paintings-on-the-wall kind – she also had the idea to have our show under people's drinks. In other words, our art works would double as coasters. So we each made 50 coaster-sized art works, tagged them with our website and asked Cynthia's Cyberbar to use them one night as coasters.

Not long after that we had a museum show (at what was then the Fuller Art Museum), which was a bit weird because now the museum was doing everything, deciding what would be shown, writing the press releases, designing the invites and the like. All the things we normally did. So I asked the curator Denise Markonish, what should we do? To which she said, "Why not have another coaster project?" To which I replied, "Great idea, let's invite the whole world." Which, in our own way, we did.

This was during the early days of the Internet, in 2000 – before spam really was an issue. So we got out the latest edition of the *Art Diary* and emailed everyone in it. And, in a short time, over 100 artists signed up to participate, meaning that they had to make 100 coaster-sized art works, agree to show a set of all the participating artists' similarly coaster-sized works in a public space and then give the works away for free. I'll never forget, one day I received a packet from Ticino, where J & W Management (Maria Walther and Patricia Jacomella) staged their exhibit. I had to read it over twice. At the end of their coaster give-away, they wrote that Harald Szeemann took the remaining ones for his collection. I can't think of a greater honor.

Oh! and, about the seven continents – that really was thanks to one of the other organizers, Ted Cantrell. He really wanted the project in Antarctica, so he managed to get a group a people to distribute them on board their ship stationed there.

The Coaster Project was really an amazing event. Not only did we give away more than 10,000 artworks around the globe and stage 100 exhibitions on seven continents in a three month period, but many of the artists actually started their own spin-off projects. It wasn't long then before the question of what the next project would be arose, which led to the creation of *The Tile Project, Destination: The World* followed by *Here, There and Everywhere*, and on and on...

INTERVIEW

What prompted the International Conference on Opportunities in the Arts, which is how I first learned of TransCultural Exchange?

Well, although *The Tile Project* attracted some major support – for instance, from the United Educational, Scientific and Cultural Organization (UNESCO), the Open Society Network and Asian Cultural Council – it now had become much more commonly accepted for artists to be staging their own shows. So, in a way, just to do a show in one place or another was becoming less interesting.

Also around the same time as *The Tile Project*, I was invited to be an artist in resident at various places, including at MIT. (MIT's glass lab actually participated in *The Tile Project*.) When I told friends of these marvelous places I'd been to as a consequence, most said that they wanted to go there as well. So I had an idea: what if TransCultural Exchange invited some residency directors here to meet them? And that's just what we did – and have been doing since 2007.

And your own studio work? Was this impinging on it?

On the contrary! Just as writing about artworks made me more critical of my own work, widened my horizons and offered me the chance to look at and think about a lot of art, TransCultural Exchange has been a positive force. I'm sure it helped me secure the Fulbright grants I received, which led to my meeting Benoit Granier, the composer I'm working with for *The Fugue*. To say nothing of the opportunity to go to Sarajevo, where I had the most amazing experience attending a Sufi ceremony, or of flying over Boston in a helicopter.

Through TransCultural Exchange I have met fantastic people. Indirectly, it was how I met Florian Grond who did the sonfication for *Delay* and Yannick Franck, the composer for two other pieces of mine. And what so pleases me about TransCultural Exchange is how many others have had similar experiences.

I know many people complain about the art world, its hype, its this or that... none of this really bothers me. It is what it is and to some extent has always been. I'm much more interested in what other possibilities exisit and in exploring those.

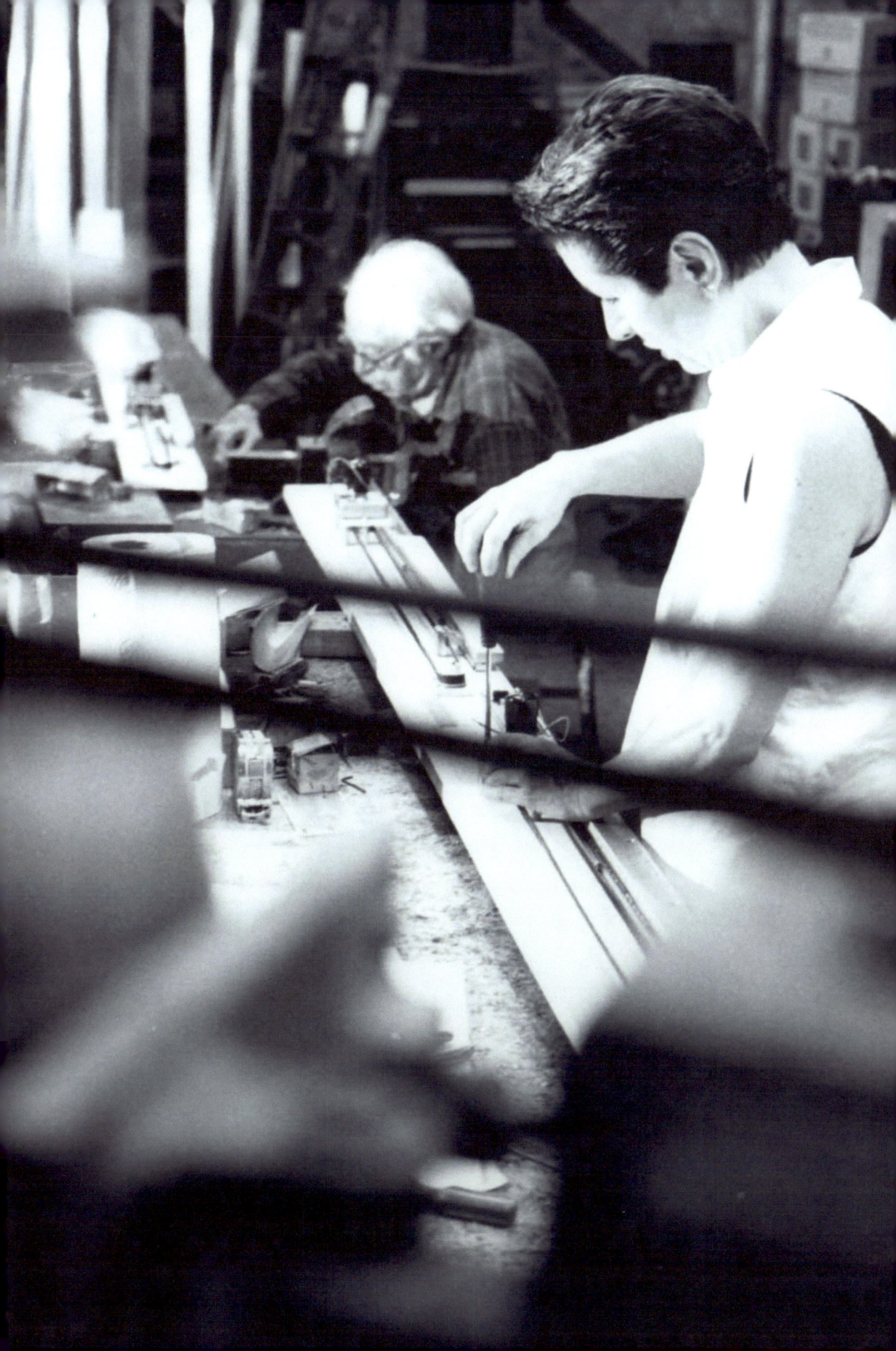

SHOOTING FOR THE STARS

Taipei

Oil paint on wood, aluminum, reed sensor and flashing red light

14¾" × 7" × 3"

2008

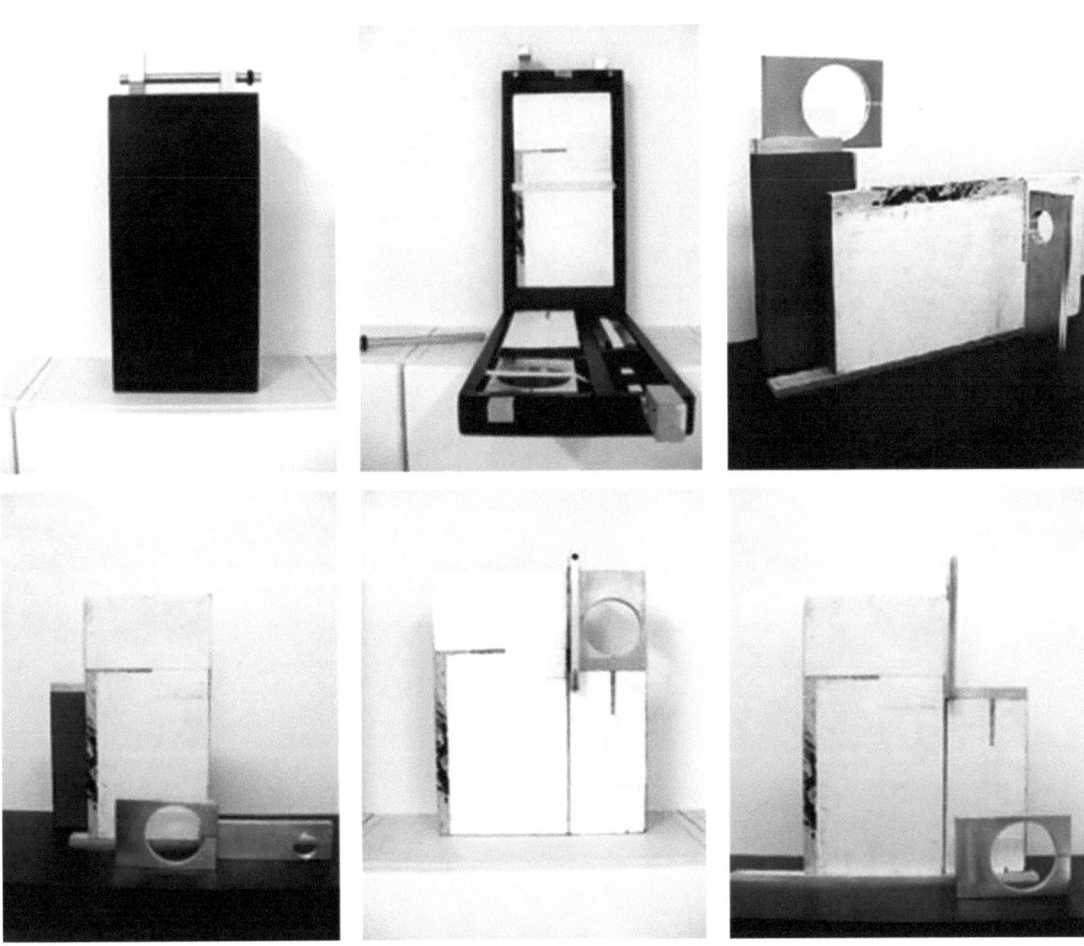

DESCRIPTION

Taipei is a multi-paneled painting that comes with its own carrying case. You can take it with you and set it up wherever you find yourself. It is, thus, something familiar – something to accompany you like a favorite accessory. And, like yourself, it can be changed and adapted to any new surrounding and then packed away to sparkle in another.

Inside the case are five discrete, painted components that can be endlessly configured and re-composed. Also embedded in the largest panel is a flashing red light that suggests Taipei's neon skyline, with its white tiled buildings and urban flavor, by day and by night (represented, respectively, by the white- and blue-sided elements).

ACKNOWLEDGEMENTS

George Bossarte for the LED circuitry.

EXHIBITION VENUES

The Isabella Stewart Gardner Museum, Boston (as a host for Lee Mingwi's *Living Room* project), 2012

Boston Sculptors Gallery, Boston, MA, *Transformers*, curated by Jane Ingram Allen, 2009

PRESS

McQuaid, Cate. "Various Evidence of Enigma." *The Boston Globe*, July 22, 2009.

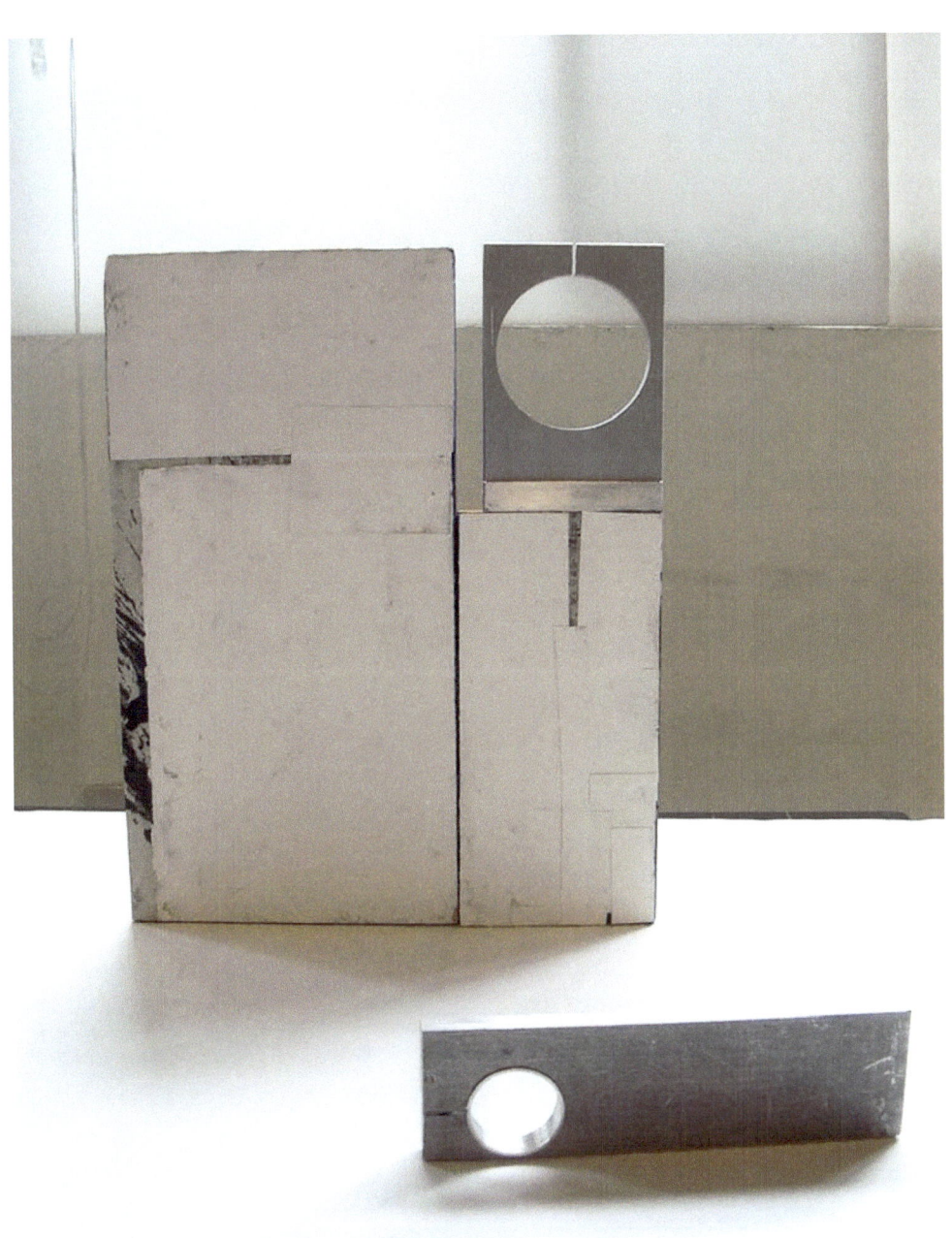

Mechanical Universe, Part I: The Pastoral

Cyber insects (by Rudi Punzi), oil paint on wood, aluminum, steel brackets, motors and electronics

Each individual 'box': 7¼" × 25" × 16"

Video documentation: https://vimeo.com/125039405

2007

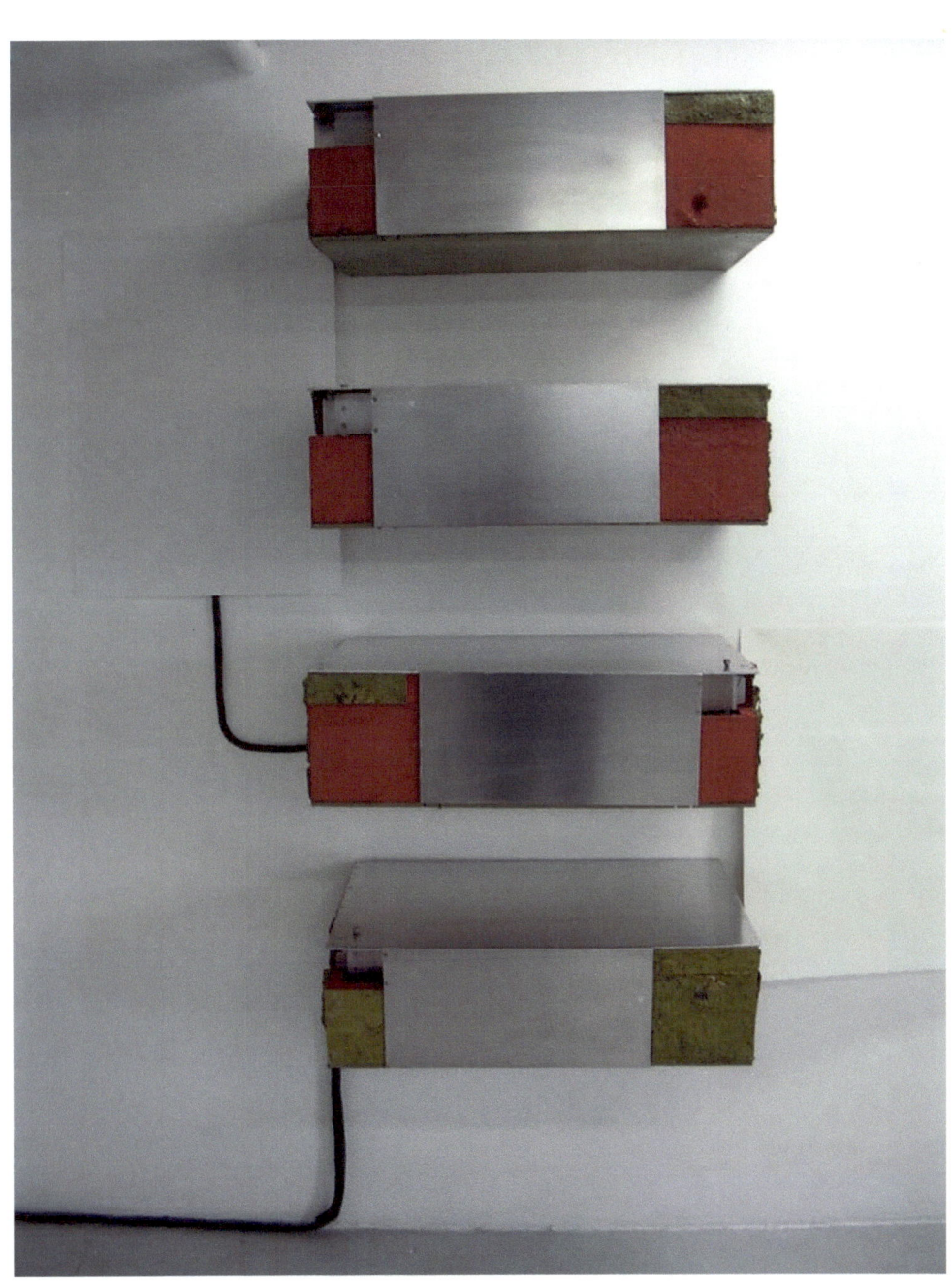

MECHANICAL UNIVERSE, PART I: THE PASTORAL

DESCRIPTION

Each "box" is a collage of highly textured paint and polished aluminum. Stepping on a button causes the doors to open at staggered intervals, revealing a host of musical "cyber insects," before slamming closed. The individual "boxes" can also be re-configured to respond to the architecture of the space in which the piece is exhibited. The idea is to create an updated, modular version of the 17th century Italian pastoral by way of the 21st century.

Mechanical Universe was created for the Boston Cyberarts Festival. The Italian artist Rudi Punzo shipped his cyber insects to the Boston, where Sherman created their living spaces – part irreverent homage to Donald Judd; part reverent homage to Jean Tinguely and Alexander Calder. But pure Punzo and Sherman.

ACKNOWLEDGEMENTS

George Bossarte for the circuitry.

EXHIBITION VENUES

Axiom Gallery, Boston, MA, 2009

Boston Sculptors Gallery, Boston, MA, 2008

Boston Cyberarts Festival, Boston, MA, *Mechanical Universe* (collaboration with Rudi Punzo, Italy), 2007

PRESS

"COLLISION14: *pov* at Axiom Gallery in Jamaica Plain." *Neighbors* TV, 2009.

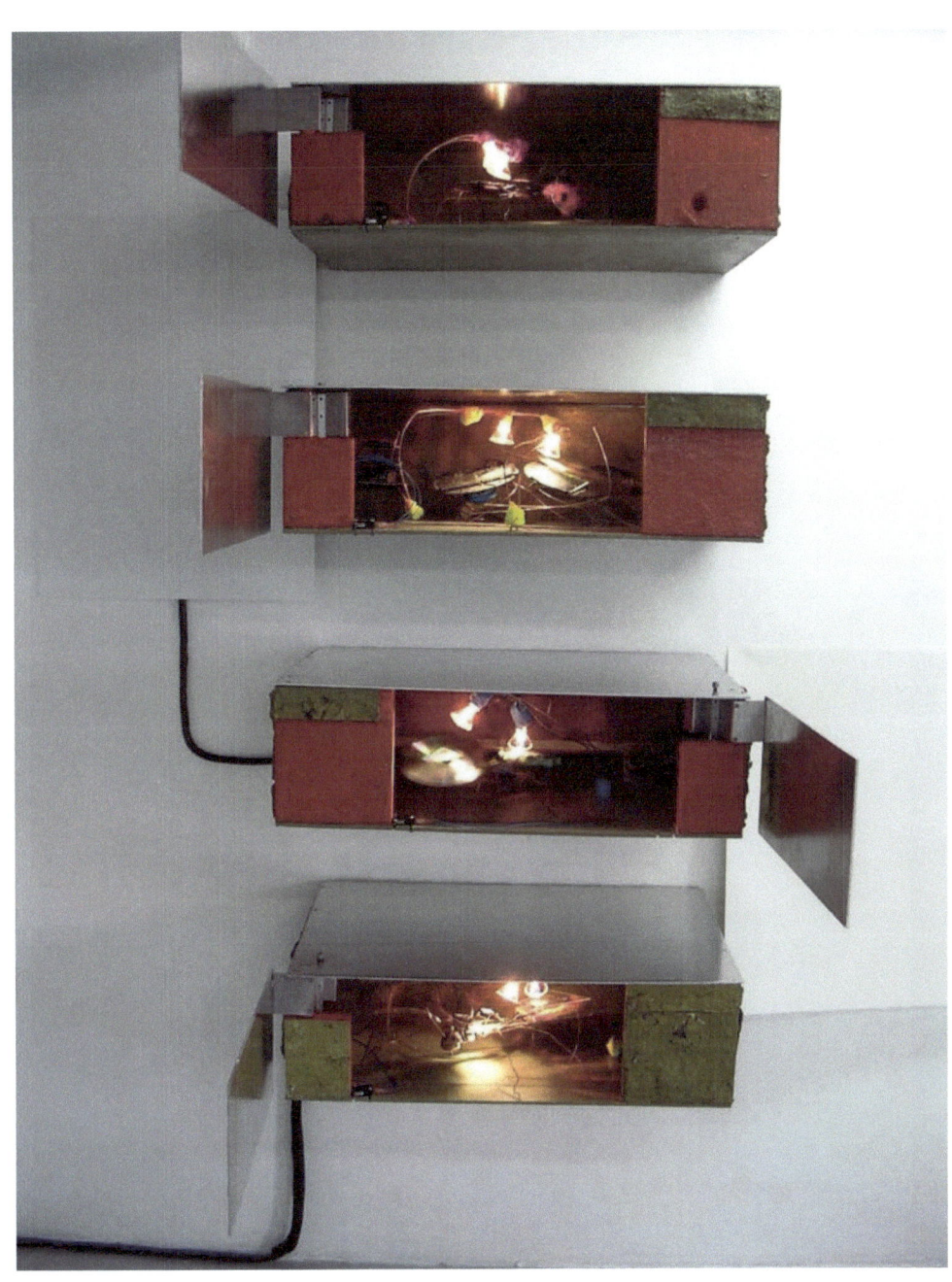

STARS

Lunker Lights ® (glow-in-the-dark fishing lures)

Dimensions variable

September 11, 2011

DESCRIPTION

This sky "painting" was created by hanging 43 extra celestial orbs (Lunker Lights ®) on tree branches (40–60' off the ground) and then inviting people to a viewing – a twilight picnic-hunt for stars, divining new constellations, telepathing moon messages to lost friends and distant lovers, remembering:

> Two armies fight throughout the day,
> The battle growing fiercer every hour,
> But when night's darkness covers them,
> Both sleep together in one bed.

- "Night 13," from *1001 Arabian Nights: Tales of 1001 Nights, Volume 1, Nights 1 to 294*, translated by Malcolm C. Lyons (Penguin Classics), p. 85.

Legend: Stars courtesy of Mary (43 Lunker Lights ®); remaining stars courtesy of the cosmos
Latitude 42° N; Longitude 71° W; West Tisbury, Martha's Vineyard, Massachusetts, USA

Remote Controlled Shooting Stars

Lexan, LEDs, push button, circuitry and paper

14" × 6½" × 6½"

2005

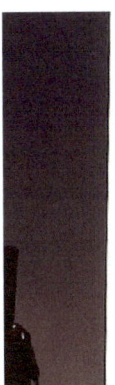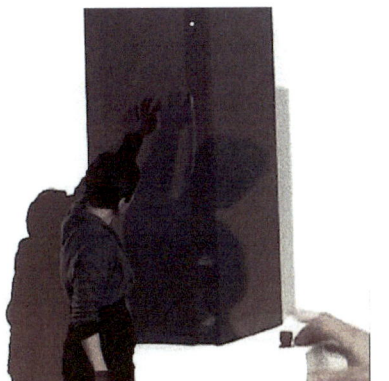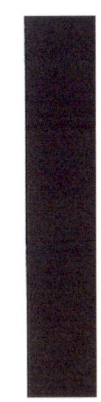

Remote Controlled Shootings Stars shown on the projection screen during Sherman's lecture at the Norwegian University of Science and Technology, Trondheim, Norway, 2013.

DESCRIPTION

Made for the show *dimensions variable; site fixed*, [1] *Remote Controlled Shooting Stars* is a model for an imaginary public artwork sited for the evening sky above Eero Saarinen's MIT Chapel. Thus, inside a black, rectangular interior is a replica of the Saarinen building, mounted on a white, wooden base. Also on the base is a red button. Pushing the button causes a small LED to drop down from the box's ceiling cluster of other tiny LEDs (meant to be "read" as a starlit sky), mimicking what the proposed remote controlled shooting stars would do.

Remote Controlled Shooting Stars, however, is not meant to be realized as an actual public artwork. To do so would turn it into a technological gee-gawk, robbing it of its model-like charm. Instead, it was conceived to be a fanciful concept, meant to complement the romantic reflections of the sky in the chapel's surrounding watery moot and the twinkling effects of Harry Bertoia's interior sculpture. And – for those who believe in astrology – to playfully suggest a way to best the gods by re-arranging the heavens and, by extension, our destinies.

ACKNOWLEDGEMENTS

George Bossarte for the circuitry.

EXHIBITION VENUES

Boston Sculptors Gallery, Boston, MA., 2011

Cambridge Arts Council, Cambridge, MA, *dimensions variable: site fixed*, 2005

PRESS

McQuaid, Cate. "Dream Projects." *The Boston Globe*, December 23, 2005.

Smyth, Amanda. "Artists' Dreamscape Builds on MIT." *MIT Tech Talk*, November 16, 2005.

Zhao, Ye. *"Dimensions Variable: Site Fixed."* World Journal, November 13, 2005.

REFERENCES AND NOTES

1. Mary Sherman, *dimensions variable, site fixed*, CAC Gallery, Cambridge, Massachusetts, 2005, press release:

    What: *dimensions variable; site fixed* (art exhibition)

    Where: CAC Gallery, Cambridge Arts Council, 334 Broadway, Cambridge, MA

    When: November 3–December 29, 2005, opening November 3, 5:30–7:30

    Who: 19 local and international artists, including the legendary artist collective Ant Farm's historical "National Sofa Project," Caroline Anderson (US) + Chingiz Babaev (Azerbaijan), Ralph Brancaccio (France), Mary Elizabeth van der Cross (US), Chu Teh-I (Taiwan), Margaret Cogswell (US), Dorothea Fleiss (Romania/Germany), Jin Soo Kim (South Korea/US), Peter Lindenmuth (US), Jannis Markopoulos (Germany), Pan Ping-Yu (Taiwan), Rudi Punzo (Italy), Urban Ramstedt (Sweden), Carlos Rodal (Mexico), Mary Sherman (US, curator), TEVAUHA (Germany), Filippos Tsitsopoulous (Spain), Ean White (US) and by special arrangement Ant Farm.

    How: By any means imaginable.

    Why: Because dreaming is a terrible thing to waste.

    OK. OK. Money is always a problem. . . technology is never quite up to snuff; but what about dreaming something up anyway?

    What about dreaming up a new artwork for Cambridge? An artwork for which money is no object. . .and technical problems are a thing of the past?

    What would you propose to create then? That was the question put to 19 local and international artists.

    The dimensions for their proposed creation could be variable, ranging from inches to meters; from two to four dimensions, but the site was fixed – Cambridge, home of the Cambridge Arts Council, known for its commissions of public work.

    The resulting "dream" works range from a tree that alters your sense of space (TEVAUHA), a sidewalk that opens up to a bandstand for street musicians (Peter Lindenmuth), a gold lamé sweater that conceals Harvard University's Science Center (Mary Elizabeth van der Cross), an operatic display of fireworks for the Charles River (Ean White), robotic insects for musical sculptures (Rudi Punzo), to a re-arrangement of the stars above MIT's Chapel (Mary Sherman).

    In some cases, the artists tackle the timely topics of politics and greed (Ralph Brancaccio, Caroline Anderson and Chingiz Babaev); in others, they propose more aesthetic responses to the cityscape (Urban Ramstedt, Pan Ping-Yu, Jin Soo Kim and Carlos Rodal); while in still others, they reconsider the nature and materials of their Cambridge locale (Dorothea Fleiss, Chu Teh-I, Margaret Cogswell, Jannis Markouplous and Filippos Tsitsopoulous).

    The Result: A fascinating reconstruction of unbuildable possibilities.

    Through the generosity of Ant Farm's Chip Lord and Media Burn Independent Video Archive, *dimensions variable; site fixed* is also pleased to include Doug Michels' visionary works *The National Sofa Project Press Conference* (filmed by Eddie Becker) and *Money Man Monument* as historical antecedents to the show's works.

Light Shade Modulator

Inkjet print on foam core and graphite on paper

4 parts:
25" x 31"
25" x 9"
25" x 9"
6" x 9"

2015

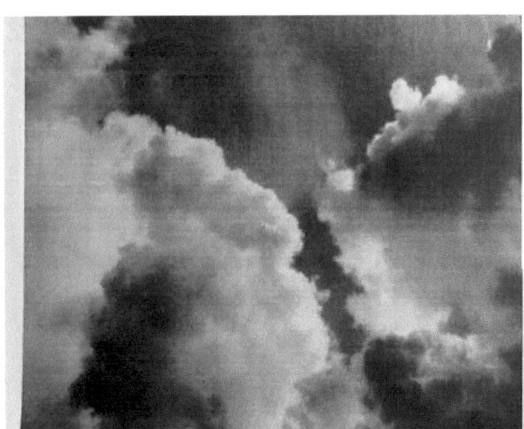 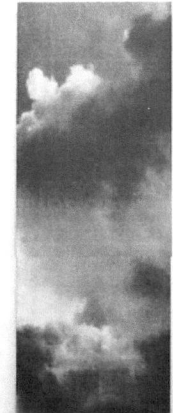 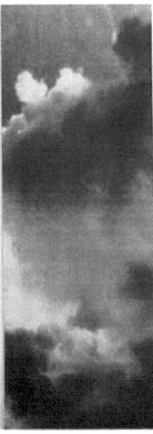 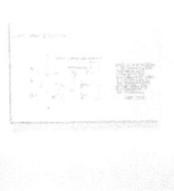

DESCRIPTION

Light Dark Modulator was created for the exhibition *Understanding Means Reducing*.[1] For that show, artists were invited to create works that underscore the notion that an art-work is the result of a period of time spent attempting to come to grips with something, which is then winnowed down and presented to an audience. With that in mind, *Light Dark Modulator* touches upon the common urge to try to understand the world by considering some aspect of it through the process of replication.

The main part of *Light Dark Modulator* consists of three black and white Xeroxes that recall Félix González Torres' give-away posters of clouds, reconfigured to also reference frames of a film. They depict the passing of time, now lost. All that remains is this distilled memento and its hints of others. In addition, there is a schematic drawing, which functions as a kind of wall label. It depicts a circuit that reacts to light and dark situations, mimicking the function of clouds. The title is meant to call to mind Moholy-Nagy's *Light-Space Modulator*, also known as the *Light Prop for an Electric Stage*, and its production of an ever-changing interplay of lights and shadows as depicted in the film *Lichtspiel Schwarz-Weiß-Grau (Light Play Black-White-Grey)*, directed by Moholy-Nagy in 1931.

EXHIBITION VENUE

Eugenia Gortchakova, *Understanding Means Reducing*, Elisabeth-Anna-Palais, Oldenburg, Germany, 2015.

REFERENCES AND NOTES

1. Eugenia Gortchakova, *Understanding Means Reducing*, Elisabeth-Anna-Palais, Oldenburg, Germany, 2015, press release:

    > To understand the world means to reduce its fullness. Art is such a process: as well as understanding art is also searching externally given perceptible signs for an insight. An artist reduces (simplifies, shortens, compresses, renounces, does without spatial or temporal distance...) until he/she finds the expression in which he/she recognizes his/her idea, intention and thus understands himself/herself for the first time.
    >
    > The exhibition will present art works in which different types of reduction are applied – from geometric and minimalist compositions up to the use of language in visual poetry. Thus the perspective on art as a means of understanding will become evident, directing the viewer to search for insight, for his/her own singular way.

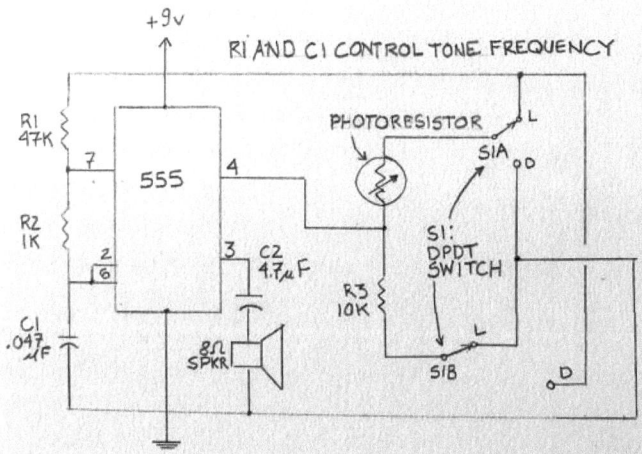

When S1 is in position "L", the speaker emits a tone when light illuminates the photoresistor. When S1 is in position "D," the speaker emits a tone when the photoresistor is NOT illuminated.

Sound, Images and Data: All Dressed up and Ready to Go (A Cautionary Tale)

by Mary Sherman

Linking the words "Sound, Images and Data" automatically sets up a connection between the three. And certainly that makes sense. Ever since the computer came to dominate our lives, all three have been adapted, augmented, challenged and changed by that ubiquitous device. Many things that could not be done – or done with great difficulty (such as light shows for rock concerts and Robert Rauschenberg's 1966 tennis game for 9 *Evenings: Theatre and Engineering*) [1] are now a snap. Life without computers and their translation of the world into inputs and outputs, into ones and zeros now seems light-years away.

Most ways that digitalization has been embraced in the last decades, however, seem odd. [2] All the number crunching, translation of data into easily digestible graphs, sound into colored charts, experiences into video and the like, has resulted in a shrinking down, flattening and smoothing out or, in the case of 3D simulators, compression of our actual world, even though, for instance, the experience of video is far less richly textured, nuanced and, arguably, compelling than film. And, of course one could claim the same about digital sound versus vinyl recordings, versus a concert hall performance.

I often wonder: what psychological shift prompted this appeal for instant access over enhanced quality? This sensual aversion and retreat? To me, all this steamrolling of our world seems very strange. Shouldn't it be the reverse? Didn't *Star Trek* promise inter-galactic travel? What happened to being beamed up? I, for one, will feel very sad if the future promises that I get all dressed up for a night in the city of lights and only a virtual version of me can instantly be teleported to Paris, but not me myself! No matter how faithful a resolution of the Mona Lisa, no number of pixels will turn that icon into the same experience as seeing the painting. It will always remain like that photo of your best friend on your smartphone – hardly the same. [3]

Moreover, the last decades' mania for digitalizing every possible experience seems to negate the greatest discoveries of the modern world: that the world is round, not flat; [4] that the universe is multi-dimensional and a vast amount of it exists beyond

SID
SOUNDS, IMAGES AND DATA CONFERENCE
23—25 JULY 2015
NEW YORK UNIVERSITY, STEINHARDT SCHOOL

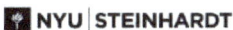 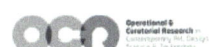 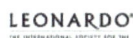

Excerpt from the talk of the same title at New York University's Steinhardt School as part of SID, Sound, Images and Data Conference, July 23–25, 2015.

SOUND, IMAGES AND DATA: ALL DRESSED UP AND READY TO GO (A CAUTIONARY TALE)

our immediate grasp. Hundreds of wavelengths pass by all the time but aren't readily perceptible. Thus, there is a huge amount of data – sounds, colors and other inputs – bombarding us all that time that definitely effects us, but also eludes us. Of course, how can this be surprising? We spend lifetimes trying to know our parents, children and partners and never really manage. People we know intimately – down to their sight, touch, even smell; day in and day out – I dare say still manage to surprise us. In other words, data can be useful, technology can be useful, hearing something beyond the auditory range can be useful; but one of the most wonderful things about being human remains: being in the world and interacting with the world. Hence the subtitle to this paper: "A cautionary tale." Wonder, surprise, love, desire – all the things that compel us – are very much related to the haptic, to our physical sense of being in the world. They are the magic of life as much as of art. Or, as the brilliant poet Byron so aptly noted, I quote:

> He thought about himself, and the whole Earth,
> Of Man the wonderful, and of the Stars,
> And how the deuce they ever could have birth;
> And then he thought of Earthquakes, and of Wars,
> How many miles the Moon might have in girth,
> Of Air-balloons, and of the many bars
> To perfect Knowledge of the boundless Skies;
> And then he thought of Donna Julia's eyes.

– George Gordon Byron, *Don Juan* (1898), Canto 1, stanza 92.

REFERENCES AND NOTES

1. *9 Evenings: Theatre and Engineering* took place from October 13th–23rd, 1966 at New York's 69th Regiment Armory. Conjured up by the artist Robert Rauschenberg and Bell Labs Engineer Billy Klüver, the event was a technological gesamtkunswerk that, in typical Wagnerian fashion, stretched over days. It was a baroque dream come true. Instead of ceilings and walls painted so realistically as to suggest the views they blocked, infrared detectors showed what we could not see in the dark. Memory palaces were replaced by sound waves, and automatons were directed by walkie-talkies. The only problem was that the technology was not quite up to the task – nor, probably, was the artistry. Many of the artists, such as Rauschenberg, later abandoned the use of technology in their work.

2. How well the computer – no matter how large the data sample – has the ability to accurately predict such things as future trends remains questionable. Weather prediction – which is probably one of the best examples of fairly reliable data analysis – is still quite fallible. No one (that I'm aware of) forecasted the Japanese tsunami. And when a group of trend predictors tried to use Twitter posts to determine the outcome of the Academy Awards, they failed as miserably as any bookie using past performances to predict the outcome of a race.

    Some things just happen. And, if we continually imagine that the past can reliably predict the future, we miss out on the things in the so-called proverbial left field, where some of our greatest discoveries reside. After all, nature tends to favor variety. It is not the strains that evolve slowly over time that one has to look out for, but the rare mutations that pop-up out of seemingly nowhere that alter the course of history.

3. At the same time, though, I am very much advocating for artists to embrace technology. One of the reasons painting has survived so long is because it is a resilient medium, informed and responding to the advances of its age. And today that means grappling with the digital world. Somehow, though, the result was that painting got translated into pixels; and paint – with all its wonderful physical dimensionality – got sucked up, like most objects now, into a virtual vacuum.

4. The mania that led to otherwise serious venues like concert halls spending time and money to create Second City clones is nothing short of a tale straight out of Lewis Carroll's *Alice in Wonderland*, or, more precisely, his later *Sylvie and Bruno* (or, if one prefers, Jorge Luis Borges' "On Exactitude in Science"), where the inhabitants make a marvelous map. It was a 1:1 scale map of the world! But as one of characters notes, it was a bit impractical, so "we now use the country itself, as its own map, and I assure you it does nearly as well."

Caller ID

Smartphone screenshot

3" × 2"; composite image: 24" × 17"

2016

CALLER ID

DESCRIPTION

This piece was made for TransCultural Exchange's contribution to the Herter Gallery's *50 Shades of Red* exhibition. For this project (inspired by the artist Thad Beal's own smart phone display), TransCultural Exchange tapped into its international network, asking people to photograph their fingerprint – i.e., to put their finger over the lens of their smartphone, snap a picture of it and send the resulting photo to TransCultural Exchange to be made into a grid of photos. (In other words, a composite, photographic collage – a color directory of each participant's phone contact.) Surprisingly, all the results were red – 50 unique shades of red, to be exact.

EXHIBITION VENUE

50 Shades of Red, Herter Gallery, University of Massachusetts, Amherst, 2016

Lanfranco Aceti, Rome, Italy	Zeerak Ahmed, Karachi, Pakistan	Lynne Allen, Boston, MA	Gulay Alpay, Istanbul, Turkey	Mikki Ansin, Cambridge, MA	Karl Baden, Boston, MA	Alberto Balestrieri, Montreal, Canada	Tommy Barr, Belfast, Northern Ireland	Thad Beal, Boston, MA	Ralph Brancaccio, London, England
Blake Brasher, Cambridge, MA	Jean-Yves Coffre, Marnay-sur-Seine, France	Michaela Davies, Sydney, Australia	Mario Diacono, Boston, MA	Florian Dombois, Zurich, Switzerland	Jeneil Engelstad, Seattle, WA	Marlene Ghormley, McClean, VA	Eugenia Gortchakova, Oldenburg, German	Benoit Granier, Beijing, China	Jude Griffin, Salem, MA
Florian Grond, Montreal, Canada	Michael Gurran, Boston, MA	Brunhild Hansen-Schmidt, Gitschenen, Switerland	Katherine Higgins, Boston, MA	M.K. Ho, Chiayi City, Taiwan	Sarah Holt, Boston, MA	Roland Idaczyk, Wellington, New Zealand	Ozlem Kalkan Erenus, Istanbul, Turkey	Janna Longacre, Brookline, MA	Eva Lundsager, Boston, MA
Dyan Marie, Toronto, Canada	Liz Marren, Boston, MA	Johannes Michler, Kiel, Germany	Regina Maria Moeller, Singapore	Ping-Yu Pan, Taipei, Taiwan	Bojana Panevska, Strasbourg, France	Janna Powell, Boston, MA	Rudi Punzo, Turin, Italy	Brian Reeves, Boston, MA	Don Ritter, Hong Kong
Malvina Sammarone, São Paulo, Brazil	Michael Schwab, London, England	Taylor Scott, Hamilton, New Zealand	Mary Sherman, Boston, MA	Andrei Sicoldi, Innsbruck, Austria	Karola Teschler, Velbert, Germany	TEVAUHA, Nürnberg, Germany	Joe Uphsm, Brookline, MA	Catheline van den Branden, Boston, MA	Siyi Wang, Dalian, China

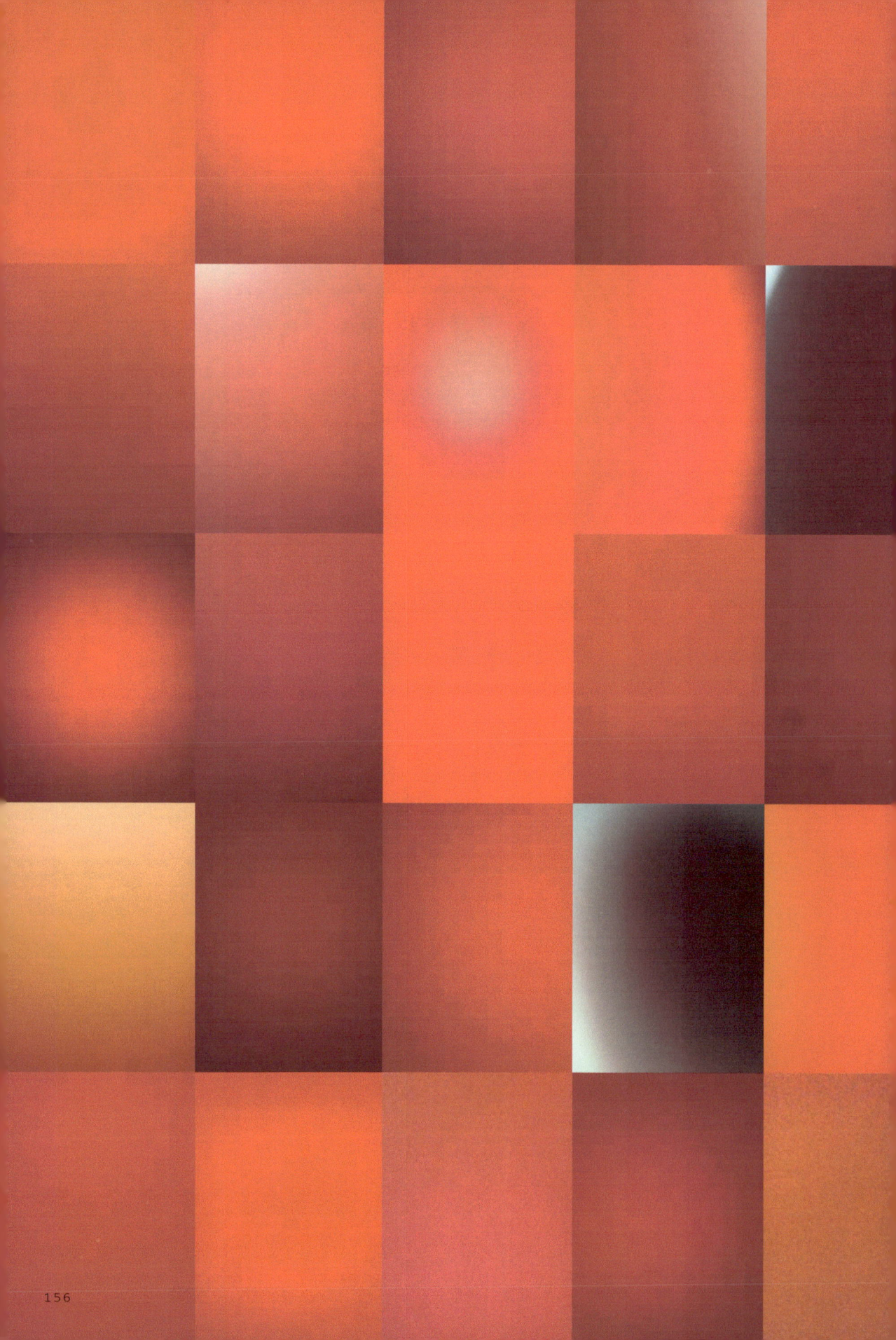

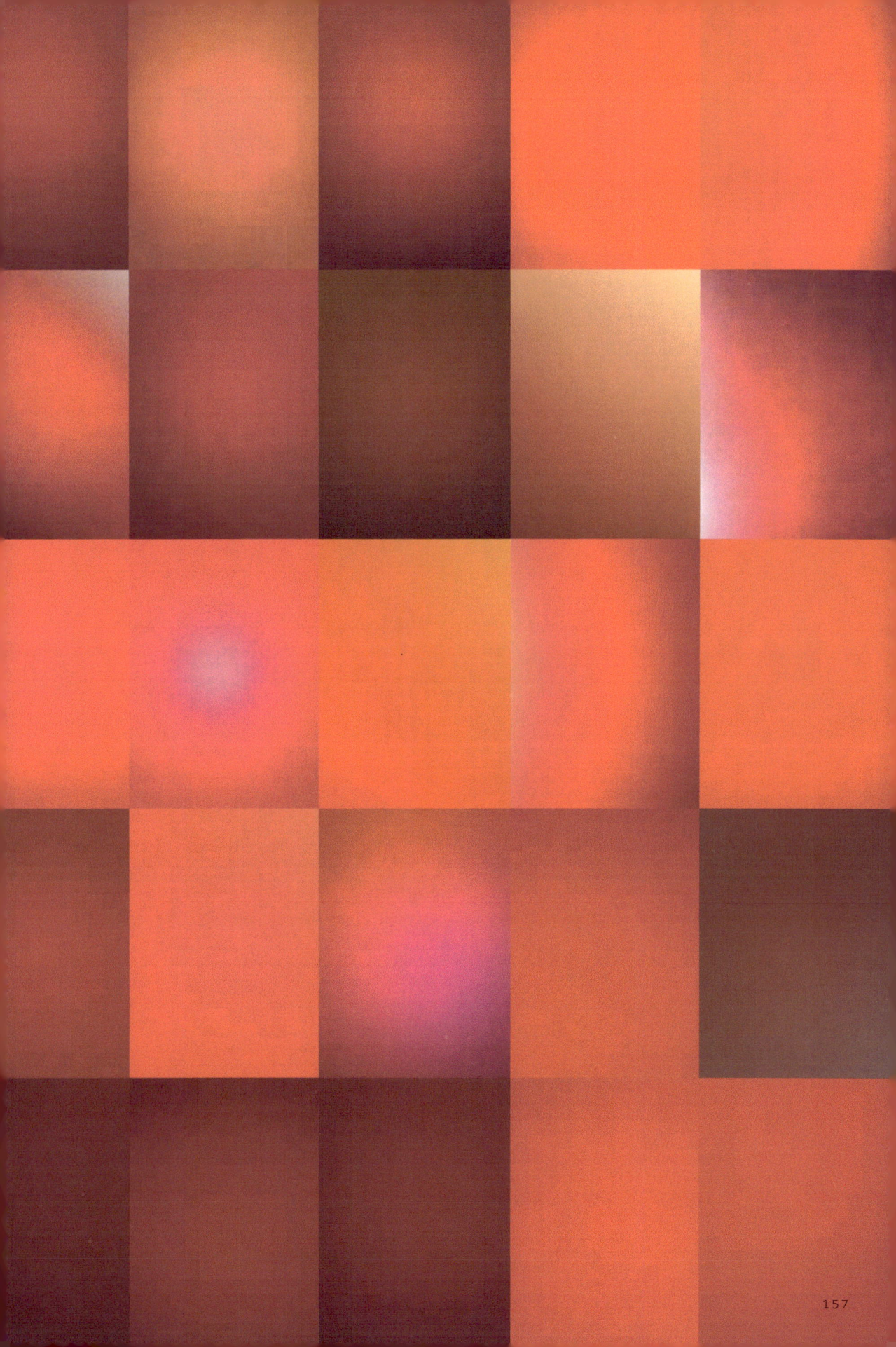

APPENDIX

Appendix

In the year 2000, the artist collaborative TransCultural Exchange launched its first *Coaster Project* at the 2000 London Biennale, followed by a second, global version in conjunction with their show in 2002 at New York City's Trans Hudson Gallery and a 10th anniversary of the project at Toronto's 2012 BIG on Bloor Festival. For the first version, the members of TransCultural Exchange made artworks in the form of coasters that were exhibited and then distributed, free of charge, under unsuspecting patron's drinks at London's Cynthia's Cyberbar and New York's Telephone Bar. What followed next was TransCultural Exchange's first truly, global art project. Using the then-fledgling Internet, TransCultural Exchange solicited artists around the world to participate in *The Coaster Project, Destination: The World*. The result: between March 9 and May 19, 2002, 99+ artists transcended geographical, political and cultural boundaries to stage 99+ exhibitions throughout the world. Afterwards, all 10,000+ artworks were given away in the guise of "coasters" at bars, cafes and restaurants.

The Coaster Project, Destination: The World was later followed by numerous other global projects, including *The Tile Project, Destination: The World* and *Here, There and Everywhere: The Art of the Future*:

http://transculturalexchange.org/activities/the-tile-project/overview/

http://transculturalexchange.org/activities/here-there-future/

2000 Coaster Artists

Theodore Cantrell
Victoria Hanks
Bill Rock
Malvina Sammarone
Mary Sherman
Sunghoon Yang

2002 Coaster Project Artists

ANTARCTICA/AUSTRALIA: Theodore Cantrell
BRAZIL: Augusto Citrangulo, Fátima Neves, Malvina Sammarone
CANADA: Patrick DeCoste, Amy Harrison and Grant Wilson (collaborative team), Lee Richmond, Tracy Susheski
CHINA: Wurigendalai Bo, Moni Oolyonghai
COLOMBIA: June Blanco
DENMARK: Mie Olise Kjaergaard
ENGLAND: Vivienne Edward Birt
FINLAND: Pirjo Heino
FRANCE: Ralph G. Brancaccio, Doris Kloster
FRENCH WEST INDIES, FRANCE: Anne Lilly
GERMANY: Michael Gould, Wolfgang Jeske, Jannis Markopoulos, Sasha Schwartz, Angelika Wolf
INDIA: Bharati Kapadia, Nina Sabnani
IRELAND: Bernie Laherty
ISRAEL: Karmela Berg, Neta Dor (Lemelshtrich)
ITALY: Daniele De Batté, Letizia Cariello
JAPAN: Carol Van Zandt
KOREA: Sunghae Chu, Hae Sun Hwang, Juri Kim, Yeontae Kim, Michan Na, Nashim Yang, Sunghoon Yang
MEXICO: Carlos Pez, Carlos Rodal
NEW ZEALAND: Roland Idaczyk
PALESTINE: Aissa Deebi
PHILIPPINES: Lala Gallardo, Claro Ramirez, Eric L. Zamuco
POLAND: Zbigniew Warpechowski
RUSSIA: Andrei Vovk
SCOTLAND: Barry McGlashan
SLOVENIA: Iztok Smajs Muni
SOUTH AFRICA: Wilma Cruise
SPAIN: Alberto Chinchon, Alberto de las Heras, Yolanda Moreno, Oscar Villegas Paez, Marie-Anne Verougstraete
SWEDEN: Urban Ramstedt
SWITZERLAND: J & W Management Consulting (collaborative team: Maria Walther and Patricia Jacomella)
THE NETHERLANDS: Martine Jacobs
TURKEY: Gülay Alpay

UNITED STATES
California: Leo F. Hobaica Jr., Meira Yedidsion
Colorado: Linda Foster Leonhard
Florida: Andy Fotopoulos
Illinois: Caroline Anderson, Ruby Louise Barnes and Ginny Sykes (collaborative team), Pauline Kochanski and Frank Crowley (collaborative team)
Iowa: Paul Chelstad Maine: Gabriel Kleinwald Maryland: Ruth Pettus
Massachusetts: Karl Baden, Roger Boyce, Charles Guiliano, Narinjan Khalsa, Khalid Kodi, Anne Faith LaPrade, Annette Lemieux, Elizabeth Marran, Klaus Postler, Mary Sherman
Minnesota: Janna Schneider
Nebraska: Paul Hotchkiss, Nan Wilson
New Jersey: Heejung (Hazel) Kim
New York: Joshua Deaner, Janet Echelman, Vince Garguilo, Kim Sillen Gledhill, Victoria Hanks, Stacey Lauren, Sharon Nakazato, Karen Roff, Karl J. Volk
North Dakota: Deane Colin Fay
Oklahoma: Shan Goshorn
Oregon: TJ Norris
Rhode Island: Roger Mayer
Utah: Shawn Dallas Stradley
Washington D.C.: Bill Rock

APPENDIX

DISTRIBUTION SITES

ANTARCTICA/AUSTRALIA
Davis Station, Antarctica / Information Services Section, Australian Antarctic Division, Kingston, Tasmania

BRAZIL
AM Arte Design, R. Prof. Morais, 476/loja 5, Belo Horizonte, May 7
Astor Bar R. Delfina, 163, Vila Madalena, May 7

CANADA
The Arabesque Restaurant, 43 Maple Street, Barrie, Ontario, May 13–19
Cameron House, 408 Queen Street West, Toronto, Ontario, March 17
Havana Gallery and Havana Restaurant, 1212 Commercial Drive, Vancouver, March 29–31
The Paddock, 178 Bathurst Street, Toronto, March 15

CHINA
The Arch Bar and Cafe as part of Zendai Museum of Modern Art's series of public art programs *Intrude*, 439 Wukang Rd. corner, Changning District, Shanghai, China, 200052, February 2008
Inner Mongolia Museum of Fine Arts, Inner Mongolia, Huhhot City, March 10
Inner Mongolia University, Academy of Fine Arts Gallery, Inner Mongolia, Huhhot, March 9

COLOMBIA
Proyecta, Calle 79B No. 8–11 Local 10, Bogota

DENMARK
Svineriet, Mejlgade 36 St., Arhus C, May 4

ENGLAND
Art Legacy, 95 High Street, Odiham, Hampshire

FINLAND
Hameenlinna Art Museum, Viipurintie 2, Hameenlinna, April 6

FRANCE
Doctors without Borders reception
Le Terroir, 11 Blvd Arago, Paris, March 26

FRENCH WEST INDIES, FRANCE
Le Petit Club, Gustavia, St. Barth's, March 22

GERMANY
BOMA (BarOfModernArt), Neue Schönhauser Str. 10, Berlin, March 9
Cafe Addesso, Callinstrasse 8, Hannover, April 7
Cafe Mezzo, Lister Meile 4, Hannover, April 30
Notenkiste, Schneiderberg 7, Hannover, April 7
Zoozie's, Baldeplatz Gastronomie Gmbh, Wittelsbacherstrasse 15, Munich, March 23

INDIA
Alliance Francais Cafe, Alliance Français of Ahmedabad, Opp. Gujarat College, Vir Kinariwala Marg, Ellisbridge, Ahmedabad, April 15
Lakeeren Gallery, 185, S.V. Road, Vile Parle (W), Mumbai, April 28

IRELAND
Geoff's Cafe Bar, 9 John Street, Waterfood, May 4

ISRAEL
Cinemateque Coffee Shop, Tel-Aviv Cinemateque, Shprinzak St., Tel-Aviv, May 4
The Gallery of Mizpe Hayamim, Upper Galilee, POB 27, Rosh Pina, May 5
Fattoush Cafe Gallery, 38 Karmel St, Haifa, April 5

ITALY
Ristorante Canottieri Milano, alzaia Naviglio Grande 160, Milano, May 18

JAPAN
radio:on:studio, Black Aoyama Bldg 7F, 3-2-7 Minami Aoyama, Minato-Ku Tokyo, March 23

KOREA

Chungbuk National University, Old Main Building, hungduk-gu gaeshin-dong san 48, Chungju-si, March 26

Gyunggi University, Art School BL, seodaemun-gu chungjung-ro 2ga 71, Seoul, March 9

Hansung University, Art School Building, sungbuk-gu samsun-dong 2ga 389, Seoul, March 5

Ichon Art Center, gyunggi-do saum-dong 65-1, Ichon-si, March 17

Korea University, Student Buliding, sungbuk-gu anam-dong 5ga 11, Seoul, March 20

Museum of ChungHakDae, gyunggi-do ohung-ri 432-5, Ansung-si, March 30

Sei's Studio, Gangnam-Gu Yeoksam-Dong 751-17 2FL, Seoul, March 30

MEXICO

Museo de la Ciudad, 684 Independencia St., Centro Histórico, Guadalajara, Jalisco, June 20

La Panaderia, Av. Amsterdam 159, Col. Hipdromo Condesa, Mexico DF, May 9

NEW ZEALAND

Bowens of Bowen Street, Bowens Fine Food Shop 1, Bowen House, 1 Bowen Street

Wellington (in the same building as the New Zealand Portrait Gallery & New Zealand Centre for Photography), March 15

This coincides with the final week of the 2002 International Arts Festival in Wellington

THE PHILIPPINES

Freedom Bar Cafe, 2/F Anonas Commercial Complex, Anonas Street, Project 3, Quezon City, May 14

Music Museum, 2/F Shoppesville, Greenhills Commercial Center, San Juan, May 19

The West Gallery, 3/F Glorietta 4, Makati, May 7

POLAND

Sandomierz Cultural Association, Sandomierz, June 1

RUSSIA

"Dom" Bol'shoi Ovchinnikovskii pereulok dom #24 stroieniie 4/5, Moscow, March 27

SCOTLAND

The Foyer Restaurant and Gallery, 82a Crown Street, Aberdeen, Scotland, April 9

SLOVENIA

Mladinski Center Velenje, Saleska 3, Velenje, May 18

SOUTH AFRICA

Tratorria San Lorenzo, Rivonia Santon, March 17

SPAIN

Club Arrebato, Bilbao, April 19, 2002

Cafe Bizitza, Bilbao, April 19, 2002

Casa de la Cultura de Chinchon, Ayuntamiento de Chinchon, Plaza Mayor, 3, Chinchon, April 12

Discoteca Distrito, Bilbao, April 19, 2002

Espacio F Gallery, Mercado de Fuencarral, Calle Fuencarral, 45, Planta Sotano, Madrid, March 30

Hostal Parque, Plaza del Parque, nr 4, Ibiza Baleares, April 20

Universidad de Salamanca, Salamanca

SWITZERLAND

Cafe "Chez Renata" (part of Teatro Dimitri), Canton Ticino, April 29–May 7

THE NETHERLANDS

Gemeente Den Helder, Drs. F. Bijlweg 20, Den Helder, June 1

TURKEY

Artemis Art Center, Osmanbey halaskargazi cad., Saksi I sok. 21/2, Istanbul, May 18

APPENDIX

UNITED STATES

California
410 Boyd Street, 410 Boyd Street, Los Angelos, April 4
The Studio of Meira Yedidsion, 3161/2 W. Pico Blvd., Suite 201, Los Angeles, May 19

Colorado
Elliot's Martini Bar, 234 Linden Street, Fort Collins, April 20

Florida
Lola Bar/Lounge, 247 23d Street, Miami Beach, April 6

Illinois
Oskar Friedl Gallery, 300 West Superior Street, Chicago, May 3
Red Light Restaurant, 820 West Randolph Street, Chicago, April 27
Wishbone, 1001 W Washington Street, Chicago, May 18

Iowa
Pierce Street Coffee Works, 1920 Pierce Street, Sioux City, April 27

Maine
Ri Ra Irish Restaurant and Pub, 72 Commercial Street, Portland, April 5

Maryland
Gertrude's (located at The Baltimore Museum of Art), 10 Art Museum Drive, Baltimore, MD, April 12–14

Massachusetts
Amherst Brewing Company, 24 North Pleasant Street, Amherst, May 1
ARTcetera Auction, Cyclorama, 539 Tremont Street, October 19. (All proceeds go to the AIDS Action Committee of Boston.)
Cultural Cafe at AAMARP, 76 Atherton Street, Jamaica Plain, April 28
Boston College Arts Festival, Boston College, Chestnut Hill, April 27
The Fuller Museum of Arts, 455 Oak Street, Brockton, May 17
La Veracruzana, 31 Main Street, Northampton, April 4
mfafirstfridays, Museum of Fine Arts, Boston, 465 Huntington Avenue. Boston, April 5
Sabina Doyle's, 116 Main Street, Medway, April 15
The Java Hut, Rte. 116, Sunderland, May 1

Minnesota
Caffetto, 708 West 22nd Street, Minneapolis, May 1

Nebraska
McFoster's Natural Kind Cafe, 302 S 38th Street, Omaha, April 27
Nicholas St. Gallery @ the Hot Shops Art Center, 1301 Nicholas Street, Omaha, April 27

New Jersey
Park Pastries, 517 Washington Street, Hoboken, March 16

New York
Barrett House Art Center, 55 Noxon Street, Poughkeepsie, May 18
Boone Dog Cafe, 35 Main Street, Brewster, April 13
The Florence Lynch Gallery, New York, March 21
Galapagas Art & Performing Space, 70 N. 6th Street, Williamsburg, Brooklyn, May 10
The Half King, 505 W. 23rd St. New York, May 16
Iron Horse Tavern, Brewster, April 13
KJ's Venue, 4919 Rte 22, Amenia, May 19
The Larkin, Lark Street, Albany, April 14
New York Free Biennale, The Frying Pan, New York, April 2
Oznot's Dish, 79 Berry Street, No. 9, Williamsburg, April 6
Puck Fair, 298 Lafayette Street, New York, April 13

North Dakota
The Wonder Bar, 121 Second Street SW, Jamestown, April 12

Oklahoma
Philbrook Museum of Art, MUSE in la Villa Restaurant, 2727 S. Rockford Road, P.O. Box 52510, Tulsa, April 25

Oregon
Crush, 1412 SE Morrison Street, Portland, April 5–6

Rhode Island
Loui's Restaurant, 286 Brook Street, Providence, May 18

Utah
Red Rock Brewing Company, 254 South 200 West, Salt Lake City, March 28

Washington, D.C.
West 24, 1250 24th Street NW, April 1

GRAND FINALE: one set to be donated to the Fuller Museum of Art, along with hundreds of Massachusetts artists' single coasters to be given out at the café @ DeCordova Museum and Sculpture Park, 51 Sandy Pond Road, Lincoln, MA 01773-2600.
Beginning June 8

EXHIBITION SITES

ANTARCTICA/AUSTRALIA: Davis Station, Antarctica / Information Services Section, Australian Antarctic Division, Kingston, Tasmania

BRAZIL
AM Arte Design, R. Prof. Morais, 476/ loja 5, Belo Horizonte, April 25–May 7
Astor, Rua Delfina, 163, Vila Madalena, Sao Paulo, April 30–May 7

CANADA
The Arabesque Restaurant, 43 Maple Street, Barrie Ontario, May 6–13 (with an opening on May 6)
A.W.O.L. Gallery, 78 Ossington Avenue, 2nd Floor, Toronto, Ontario, March 7–17
Havana Gallery and Havana Restaurant, 1212 Commercial Drive, Vancouver, B.C., March 22–28
SPIN Gallery, 156-158 Bathurst Street, Toronto, Ontario, March 9–14

CHINA
The Arch Bar and Cafe as part of Zendai Museum of Modern Art's series of public art programs Intrude, 439 Wukang Rd. corner, Changning District, Shanghai, China, 200052, February 2008
Inner Mongolia Museum of Fine Arts, Inner Mongolia, Huhhot City, March 10
Inner Mongolia University, Academy of Fine Arts Gallery, Inner Mongolia, Huhhot, March 9

COLOMBIA
Proyecta, Calle 79B No. 8–11 Local 10, Bogota

DENMARK
Galerie Wolfson, Tiendêladen 6, Aalborg, April 26–28

ENGLAND
Art Legacy Ltd., 95 High Street, Odiham, Hampshire, March 9–May 19

FINLAND
Art Gallery Ripustus, Rauhankatu 11, Hameenlinna, March 9–31

FRANCE
Parsons School of Design Paris, 14, rue Letellier, Paris, March 25
UNESCO, Paris

FRENCH WEST INDIES, FRANCE
Le Resto, Gustavia, St. Barth's, March 22

APPENDIX

GERMANY
Andreas Baumgartl, Galerie fur Zeitgenoessische Kunst, Platzl 4, Munich, March 20–22
Atelier Block 16, Edwin-Oppler Weg 14, Hannover, March 31
BOMA (BarOfModernArt,) Neue Schönhauser Str. 10, Berlin, March 9
Cafe Mezzo, Lister Meile 4, Hannover, April 1–30
CEDON Museum Shops GmbH in the Hypo-Kunsthalle, Theatinerstr. 8, Munich, March 22–23
Gasthaus Pasemann, Emmer Dorfstrasse 35, Hankensbuttel, May 12–26

INDIA
Alliance Francais of Ahmedabad, Opp. Gujarat College, Vir Kinariwala Marg, Ellisbridge, Ahmedabad, April 15
Lakeeren Gallery, 185, S.V. Road, Vile Parle (W), Mumbai, April 27
The National Institute of Design, Design Gallery, Paldi Ahmedabad, March 15

IRELAND
Waterford Cineplex, Patrick Street, Waterford, March 14–31

ISRAEL
Tel-Aviv Cinemateque 2, Shprinzak St., Tel-Aviv, April 28–May 4
The Gallery of Mizpe Hayamim, Upper Galilee, POB 27, Rosh Pina, April 28–May 4
Fattoush Cafe Gallery, 38 Karmel St, Haifa, March 10–April 5

ITALY
Associazione Viafarini, Via Farini, 35, Milan, March 12

JAPAN
radio:on:studio, Black Aoyama Bldg 7F, 3-2-7 Minami Aoyama, Minato-Ku, Tokyo, March 10–23

KOREA
Chungbuk National University, Old Main Building, hungduk-gu gaeshin-dong san 48 Chungju-si, March 3–26
Gyunggi University, Art School BL, seodaemun-gu chungjung-ro 2ga 71, Seoul, March 7–9
Hansung University, Art School Building, sungbuk-gu samsun-dong 2ga 389, Seoul, March 4–5
Ichon Art Center, gyunggi-do saum-dong 65-1, Ichon-si, March 15–17
Korea University, Student Buliding, sungbuk-gu anam-dong 5ga 11, Seoul, March 3–20
Museum of ChungHakDae, gyunggi-do ohung-ri 432-5, Ansung-si, March 29–30
Sei's Studio, Gangnam-Gu Yeoksam-Dong 751-17 2FL, Seoul, March 1–30
Gallery ARTSIDE, 170 KwanHoon Dong Chongno Gu Seoul 110-300 Korea 82-2-725-1020, May 1–7

MEXICO
Museo de la Ciudad, 684 Independencia St., Centro Histórico, Guadalajara, Jalisco, May 16–June 20
La Panaderia, Av. Amsterdam 159, Col. Hipódromo Condesa, Mexico DF, May 2–9

NEW ZEALAND
Bowens of Bowen Street, Bowens Fine Food Shop 1, Bowen House, 1 Bowen Street, Wellington (in the same building as the New Zealand Portrait Gallery & New Zealand Centre for Photography), March 11–15. (This coincides with the final week of the 2002 International Arts Festival in Wellington.)

THE PHILIPPINES
Freedom Bar Cafe, 2/F Anonas Commercial Complex, Anonas Street, Project 3, Quezon City, May 14
Music Museum, 2/F Shoppesville, Greenhills Commercial Center, San Juan, May 7–19
The West Gallery, 3/F Glorietta 4, Makati, April 25–May 7

The Negros Museum, Gatuslao Street, Bacolod,
June 8–25.

POLAND
Otwarta Pracownia Gallery, ul. Dietla 11, Kracow,
April 26–May 29

RUSSIA
"Dom" Bol'shoi Ovchinnikovskii pereulok dom #24 stroieniie
4/5, Moscow, March 9–27

SCOTLAND
Foyer Gallery, Grays School of Art, Garthdee Road, Aberdeen,
April 1–8

SLOVENIA
Mladinski Center Velenje, Saleska 3, Velenje, May 17–18

SOUTH AFRICA
The Open Window Gallery, 410 Rigel Avenue, Erasmus Rand,
Pretoria, March 15–17

SPAIN
Bilbao Arte, Urazurrutia, 32, Bilbao, April 8–15
Casa de la Cultura de Chinchon, Ayuntamiento de Chinchon,
Plaza Mayor, 3, Chinchon, April 4–7
Espacio F Gallery, Mercado de Fuencarral, Calle Fuencarral,
45, Planta Sotano, Madrid, March 20–30
Hostal Parque, Plaza del Parque, no. 4, Ibiza Baleares, March
25–April 20
Universidad de Salamanca, Salamanca

SWEDEN
Osterbybruk Library, Dannemoravagen 5, Osterbybruk,
May 2–17

SWITZERLAND
Teatro Dimitri (Theatre I), Canton Ticino, March 9–
April 28

THE NETHERLANDS
Gemeente Den Helder, Drs. F. Bijlweg 20, Den Helder,
April 1–June 1

TURKEY
Artemis Art Center, Osmanbey halaskargazi cad., Saksi sok.
21/2 Istanbul, May 7–18

UNITED STATES
California
California Institute of Art , Character Animation Department,
24700 Mc Bean Parkway
Valencia, April 1–3
The Studio of Meira Yedidsion, 3161/2 W. Pico Blvd., Suite
201, Los Angeles, March 9–May 9

Colorado
The Fort Collins Museum of Contemporary Art, Old Post
Office Building, 201 S. College Avenue, Fort Collins, March
9–April 19

Florida
Lola Bar/Lounge, 247 23d Street, Miami Beach, March 29–
April 6

Illinois
Chicago Cultural Center, 78 East Washington Street, Chicago,
April 20–May 13
Judy Saslow Gallery, 300 West Superior Street, Chicago,
March 22–April 27
Wishbone, 1001 W. Washington Street, Chicago, May 14–18
Woman Made Gallery, 1900 S. Prairie Avenue, Chicago, March
15–April 26
NEW VENUE: Wood Street Gallery & Sculpture Garden, 1239
N Wood Street, Chicago, March 16–April 13

Iowa
Pierce Street Coffee Works, 1920 Pierce Street, Sioux City,
April 26–27

APPENDIX

Maine

The Maine College of Art, 522 Congress Street, Portland, March 23–30

Maryland

The Charles Theatre, 1711 North Charles Street, Baltimore, thecharles.com, April 1–7

Massachusetts:

ARTcetera Auction, Cyclorama, 516 Tremont Street, October 15–18

Barbara Krakow Gallery, 10 Newbury Street, Boston, March 16

Boston College, Bapst Library, 140 Commonwealth Avenue, Chestnut Hill, March 3–April 27

Framingham State College, Henry Whittemore Library, 100 State Street, P.O. Box 9101, Framingham, MA, March 24–April 12

The Fuller Museum of Arts, 455 Oak Street, Brockton, March 9–May 17

Gallery at AAMARP (African American Masters Artists-in-Residence Program), 76 Atherton Street, Jamaica Plain, April 26–28

New England School of Art & Design, Gallery 28, 75 Arlington Street, Boston, May 21–June 1

Northeastern University, Dept. of Art & Architecture, Ryder Hall, Boston, March 9–April 14

The Open Studios Press, 450 Harrison Avenue #304, Boston, March 26

Smith College's Museum of Art, Northampton, April 1

Bernard Toale Gallery, 450 Harrison Avenue, Boston, March 28–30

University of Massachusetts at Amherst, Central Gallery, Central Residential Area, Wheeler House, Infirmary Way, Amherst, April 27–April 30

University of Massachusetts at Amherst, Hampden Gallery, Southwest Residential Area, Hampden Commons, Amherst, April 27–30

University of Massachusetts at Boston, Healy Library Gallery, 5th Floor, 100 Morrissey Blvd., Boston, March 13

Minnesota

Walker Library, 2880 Hennepin Avenue, South Minneapolis, April 13–April 27

Nebraska

McFoster's Natural Kind Cafe, 302 S 38th Street, Omaha, April 26–27

Nicholas St. Gallery @ the Hot Shops Art Center, 1301 Nicholas Street, Omaha, April 26–27

New Jersey

Park Pastries, 517 Washington Street, Hoboken, March 9-16

New York

Barrett House Art Center, 55 Noxon Street, Pougkeepsie, May 11–18

Changing Spaces, 306 Hudson Avenue, Albany, March 9–April 13

The Florence Lynch Gallery, 147 West 29th Street, New York, March 15–21

Gallery Tonje, 4 Main Street, Brewster, March 9–April 9

Iron Horse Tavern, Main Street, Brewster, April 10–13

Oznot's Dish, 79 Berry Street, No. 9, Williamsburg, April 6

Parson's Fine Arts Gallery, 26 E. 14th Street, New York, April 28–May 5

PS 122 Gallery, 150 First Avenue, New York, March 30–April 21

Rockland Art Center, 27 Greenbush Road, West Nyack, April 6

Southeast Museum in Brewster, Main Street, Brewster, April 5–May 19

Unitarian Fellowship, 67 South Randolph Street, Poughkeepsie, March 7–10

North Dakota

The Arts Center, 115 2nd Street. SW. P.O. Box 363, Jamestown, March 16–April 12

Oklahoma

Tulsa City-County Library, 400 Civic Center, Tulsa, April 1–22

Oregon
Charlie White Gallery @ The Space, 1307 SW First Avenue, Portland, March 7–30

Rhode Island
221 Gallery, List Art Center at Brown University, Providence, May 11–17

Utah
Gay and Lesbian Community Center, 361 North 300 West, Salt Lake City, March 9–21

PRESS

INTERNATIONAL
Kapadia, Bharati. "The Coaster Project." *International Gallerie: A Journal of Ideas* 5, no. 1 (2002): p. 39.
Sherman, Mary. "The Coaster Project." *International Gallerie: A Journal of Ideas* 5, no. 1 (2002): pp. 36–38.

BRAZIL
"Llega a españa el *Proyecto Posavasos*." *Terra*, May 13, 2002.

FINLAND
Helin, Pekka. "Taidetta Arkeen," *Hämeen Sanomat*, p. 11, March 24, 2002.
"Pirjo Heino kansainväliseen näyttelyprojektinn." *Hämeen Sanomat*, p. 18, April 1, 2002.
Ninimäki, Pirjo-Liisa. "Vain baaritiski puutuu." *Hämeen Sanomat*, front page: Kultuuri, March 9, 2005.
"Pirjo Heino kansainväliseen näyttelyprojektinn." *Kaupunkiuutiset*, p. 18, March 9, 2002.
"Pirjo Heino kansainväliseen näyttelyprojektinn." *Kaupunkiuutiset*, p. 21, March 13, 2002.
"Pirjo Heino teoksia sadassa Näyttelyssä." *Kaupunkiuutiset*, March 9, 2002.

FRANCE
"*The Coaster Project, Destination: The World.*" Press release. *Palais de Tokyo*, April 2002.

ISRAEL
"The Centenary Exhibition." *The Centenary*, April 25, 2002.
"*The Coaster Project.*" *Maariv*, April 26, 2002.
"*The Coaster Project, Destination: The World.*" *Israeli Artists Online*, May 9, 2002. Accessed August 10, 2016. http://www.artistsonline.co.il/whatsnew.html.
Godine, Gil. "*The Coaster Project.*" The Jerusalem Post, March 2, 2002.
Ronas. "*Coaster Project.*" *Ha'ir*, p. 56, April 26, 2002.

JAPAN
Naumann, Peter. "*The Coaster Project, Destination: The World.*" *Tokyo Q*, March 8, 2002.

MEXICO
Canal 22. Television coverage.
"Llega a Guadalajara el *Proyecto Portavasos*." *El Informador*, front page: Artes, May 23, 2002.
Preciado, Corina. "Hacen suma de portavasos." *Mural*, May 20, 2002.
Preciado, Corina. "Va el arte hasta la cocina." *Mural*, front page: Cultura, May 20, 2002.
Vazquez, Enrique. "Una exposición que llega para quedarse." *El Informador*.

THE NETHERLANDS
"Geplaatst door; Marine Jacobs." Kunstinzicht, March 3, 2002. http://www.kunstinzicht.nl.
"International Exposite in gemeentehuis Den Helder." Gemeente Den Helder. Last updated March 1, 2002. http://www.denhelder.nl.

NEW ZEALAND
"*The Coaster Project.*" *Capital Times*, March 6, 2002.

APPENDIX

PHILIPPINES

"Lowly Coaster Becomes High Art." *The Manila Times*, April 11, 2002.

"Three Filipinos Join Cultural Exchange Program." *Malaya Living*, April 18, 2002.

"Three Cheers for the Lowly Coaster." *Village Voice*, April 18, 2002.

SOUTH AFRICA

"*Coaster Project* at the Open Window." *Artthrob* 55 (March 2002): p. 14.

SOUTH KOREA

"*The Tile Project*." *City Life Magazine*, May 5, 2002.

"*The Tile Project*." *Seoul Art Guide*, May 5, 2002.

UNITED STATES:

Colorado

Basquez, Anna Maria. "Coasters of the World." *Fort Collins Coloradoan*, pp. B6–B8, March 15, 2002.

MacMillan, Kyle. "*Coaster Project* Destined to End Up as Barroom Talk." *The Denver Post*, p. 5FF, April 12, 2002.

Illinois

"Art under Glass." *The Chicago Reader* 31, no. 26 (March 2002): p. 20.

Maryland

Shapiro, Stephanie. "There's Art to Serving a Drink." *The Baltimore Sun*, p. 1E, April 11, 2002.

Massachusetts

"@ parties." *Stuff Magazine*, p. 66, June 6, 2002.

"Art Exhibit Spans Globe." *The Allston-Brighton Tab*, May 24, 2002.

Bergeron, Chris. "Artists from FSC Take Part in Global Exhibit The Coaster Project.'" *The Daily News Tribune* (Framingham), April 7, 2002.

Crocetti, Paul. "Annual BC Arts Festival Continues to Expand." *The Heights* (Boston College), p. A4, April 23, 2002.

Edgers, Geoff. "Inventiveness Spills over in Coaster Project." *The Boston Globe*, May 30, 2002.

Giuliano, Charles. "Coast to Coaster." *Maverick Visual Arts*, March 18, 2002.

Schulze, Rob. "Coasters to Do Double Duty." *The Daily Hampshire Gazette*, March 30, 2002.

WGBH-Boston. Television coverage.

Willdorf, Nina. "Multicoasteralism." *The Boston Phoenix*, May 31, 2002.

North Dakota

Henning, Sara. "Coaster to Coaster." *The Forum*, April 28, 2002.

Oklahoma

Watts, James D. Jr. "Unexpected Art." *Tulsa World*, front page, April 3, 2002.

Utah

Stradley, Shawn Dallas. "What's Under Your Glass: *The Coaster Project*" *Artists of Utah Ezine*, April 2, 2002. Accessed August 11, 2016. http://artistsofutah.org/15Bytes/index.php/whats-under-your-glass-the-coaster-project/.

CURRICULUM VITAE

Mary Sherman is an artist whose works represent a steadfast infatuation with and investigation of painting – and, in particular, of what defines that medium. Along the way, her interests have branched out in numerous directions, never losing sight of her first love, oil paint.

Sherman has received numerous grants and awards, including two Fulbright Senior Specialist Grants (Taipei and Istanbul) and artist-in-residencies at the Massachusetts Institute of Technology (MIT), Pilchuk School of Glass and the Taipei Artist Village. Her works have been shown at numerous institutions, including Taipei's Kuandu Museum of Fine Arts, Beijing's Central Conservatory, Harvard University's Adams Art Space, Vienna's WUK Kunsthalle and New York's Trans Hudson Gallery. Alongside this pursuit, for two decades (from 1980–2000), she worked as an art critic for such publications as the *Chicago Sun-Times*, *The Boston Globe* and *ARTnews*. Since 1996, she has also taught at a variety of colleges and universities, and is currently a member of the faculty at Boston College, Northeastern University and Trans Arts Institute. In addition, she has lectured widely, including at NTU [Nanyang Technological University] Centre for Contemporary Art, Harvard University's Weatherhead Center for International Affairs, the Museum of Fine Arts, Boston, the University of Chicago, New York University, Trondheim Academy of Fine Art at the Norwegian University of Science and Technology and Goldsmith University. In 2010, she served as the interim Associate Director of the Massachusetts Institute of Technology's Program in Art, Culture and Technology.
In addition, Sherman has worked as a curator and is the founder and director of TransCultural Exchange, which has garnered support from such organizations as the United Nations Educational, Scientific and Cultural Organization (UNESCO), National Endowment for the Arts, the Massachusetts Cultural Council, Asian Cultural Council, the Elizabeth Firestone Graham Foundation, The Boston Foundation, the Mondriaan Foundation, the Netherland-American Foundation and numerous consulates. Among the shows she's curated, two have received awards from the Northeast Chapter of the International Art Critics Association.

INDIVIDUAL EXHIBITIONS (SELECTED)

2016   OBORO (as part of the 3rd International Digital Art Biennial [BIAN] and the Montreal Digital Spring 2016), Montreal, Canada, *Delay*
Drive-by Gallery, Boston, MA (January), *Waiting for Yves*
OBORO, Montreal, Canada, *Dream Mechanics/ Mécaniques oniriques*

2015   Crafton Hills College, Yucaipa, CA, *Waiting for Yves*

2014   Galleri KiT, Norwegian University of Science and Technology, Trondheim, Norway, *Delay*

2011   Boston Sculptors Gallery, Boston, MA, *Waiting for Yves*

2010   University of Massachusetts, Amherst, Hampden Gallery, Amherst, MA, *At Heart Spike Jones*

2009   Boston Sculptors Gallery, Boston, MA, *Mechanical Universe: Nocturne* (collaboration with Yannick Franck)

2008   Zendai MoMA, Shanghai, China, *Here Comes The Sun/Intrude: Art & Life 366 Project*

2007   Boston Cyberarts Festival, Boston, MA, *Mechanical Universe* (collaboration with Rudi Punzo, Italy)

2004   New England School of Art & Design, Boston, MA, *Cold Fish*

2003   Framingham State College, Framingham, MA, *Silence*

2002   Boston City Hall, Boston, MA, *Mary Sherman*

2001   Gallery X, NY, NY, *Mary Sherman: When is a Painting not a Painting*

2000   Emmanuel College, Boston, MA, *Off the Wall: Painted Constructions*

1999   District Fine Arts, Washington, DC, *Mary Sherman: An Urban Sky*

1998   Plains Art Museum, Fargo, ND, *Caroline Anderson/ Mary Sherman: Divergent Paths*
NYU's Rosenberg Gallery, NY, NY, *Dissecting the Cube* (collaboration with M.E. Alvarez)

1995   Harvard University, Adams Artspace, Cambridge, MA, *Mary Sherman: The Invisible Figure*

APPENDIX

GROUP EXHIBITIONS (SELECTED)

2016	King Street Station, Seattle, WA, *Nine Evenings Revisited*	2005	Quarantine Island, Izmir, Turkey
2015	Kunsthalle Mainz, Mainz, Germany, *Views on Mainz* (Curator: Thomas Trummer)		Cambridge Arts Council, Cambridge, MA, *dimensions variable: site fixed*
	New York University's Loewe Theater, *Electrified Data*		Artemis Art Center, Istanbul, Turkey, *International Invitational*
	Harvestworks, New York City, NY, *Sound Invasions*	2004	Museum Judetul Satu Mare, Satu-Mare, Romania
2014	Boston Sculptors Gallery, Boston, MA		East-West Gallery, The Romanian Consulate, NY, NY
2013	Beijing Forestry University, Beijing, China, *X-Dialogue, Part 2*	2003	Boston Center for the Arts, Boston, MA, *What If?*
2012	The Distillery Gallery, Boston, MA, *Between the Sheets: a look into the artist's sketchbooks*		New York Arts Magazine Gallery, NY, NY, *Drawing Conclusions*
	Beijing Central Conservatory of Music, "On Native Music," Beijing, China		Oskar Friedl Gallery, Chicago, IL
	Beijing Forestry University, Beijing, China		Artspace, New Haven, CT, *Between Fear and Freedom: Duct Tape*
2011	G.O. Gallery, University of Amherst, Amherst, MA, *Novel Idea*	2002	Art Complex Museum, Duxbury, MA, *Gadgets, Gizmos and Games*
	Boston Sculptors Gallery, Boston, MA		University of Massachusetts, Hampden Gallery, Amherst, MA, *Abstraction as Indicator*
	Distillery Gallery, Boston, MA, *10x10*		Fuller Museum of Art, Brockton, MA, *TransCultural Exchange*
2010	London Biennale, Boston (Satellite Venue)		Institute of Contemporary Art at Maine College of Art, Portland, ME, *Terrain*
	Boston Sculptors Gallery, Boston, MA, *On/Of/About Paper*		Fine Arts Building, Chicago, IL, *Ragdale's 25th Anniversary Exhibition*
	Boston Center for the Arts, Boston, MA, *Uninhibited*	2001	University of Massachusetts, Hampden Gallery, Amherst, MA, *New England/New York/New Talent*
2009	Axiom Gallery, Boston, MA		Casa Italiana Zerilli-Marimo, NY, NY, *Venice 2001*
	Boston Sculptors Gallery, Boston, MA, *Transformers*		Arlington Arts Center, Arlington, MA, *Constructions*
2008	Cushing-Martin Gallery, Easton, MA, *Move Me: Kineticism in Art*	2000	Trans Hudson Gallery, NY, NY, *TransCultural Exchange: nomads forever*
	London Biennale, London		London Biennale, London, UK, *The Coaster Project*
	Kuandu Museum of Fine Arts, Taipei, Taiwan, *Collaboration: Anticipating the Art of the Future*	1999	Kwanhoon Art Gallery, Seoul, South Korea, *nomads*
	Zendai MoMA, Shanghai, China, *Coaster Project/Intrude: Art & Life 366 Project*		Boston College, McMullen Museum of Art, Chestnut Hill, MA, *25 Years of Excellence*
2007	Takt Kunstprojektraum, Berlin, Germany, *American Dreams/When Worlds Collide*		New England School of Art & Design/ Suffolk University, Boston, MA, *Hatdance*
	University of Massachusetts, Amherst, MA, *Americaura*	1998	Trans Hudson Gallery, NY, NY, *no boundaries*
2006	Leonard's Codex Art Assemblage, Williamsburg, NY		Right Bank Gallery, Brooklyn, NY
	International Conference, Exhibition and Sports Center, Harbin, China		

1997	FPAC Gallery, Boston, MA, *Charged Spaces*
	Museum of Contemporary Art, Washington, DC
	McMullen Museum of Art, Boston College, Chestnut Hill, MA
	Stuyvesant Place, NY, NY, *someday a place*, outdoor installation
1995	Harvard University, Adams Artspace, Cambridge, MA, *Mary Sherman: The Invisible Figure*
	Attleboro Museum, Attleboro, MA, *Painters' Painters: Mary Sherman and Jacqueline Roth*
	Instituto Universitario d'Architettura di Venezia, Venice, Italy, 1975–1995, *Works in Progress*
	Springfield Museum of Fine Arts, Springfield, MA, *Springfield Art League's 76th National Exhibition* (Curator: Trevor Fairbrother)
	Oskar Friedl Gallery, Chicago, IL, *Anchorage*
1994	Oskar Friedl Gallery, Chicago, IL
1993	Mills Gallery, Boston Center for the Arts, Boston, MA, *The Drawing Show*
1992	Oskar Friedl Gallery, Chicago, IL
1991	Currier Gallery of Art, Manchester, NH, *New Artists 1991, The 3rd Gloria Wilcher Memorial Exhibition*
1990	Oskar Friedl Gallery, Chicago, IL
1989	Peace Museum, Chicago, IL, *Everyone Has the Right to...*
	WUK Kunsthalle, Vienna, Austria, *Gegenschwank*

INTERNATIONAL PROJECTS (SELECTED)

2009–11
Here, There and Everywhere: The Art of Collaboration, 100+ world sites, including Armenia's Corner of Teryan and Northen Avenue, Lebanon's Ministry of Tourism Gallery, Toronto's Function Gallery, India's Siddhartha High School in Stok, Poland's Rondo Sztuki Gallery, Russia's Tower Kronprinz, South Korea's Haslla Art World Museum, Emory University, Massachusetts College of Art and Design's Godine Gallery, the University of Massachusetts Amherst's The Hampden and Central Galleries, The Goethe Institut Boston, Nuremberg's Museum Industriekultur, Vienna's Kunstlerhaus, Tokyo's Ueno Onshi Park, Budapest's Orlay Salon, Beijing's Opera House, Puerto Rico's Muñoz Rivera Park, Palestine's Jabaliya Refugee Camp and cell phones throughout Tajikistan, among others.
http://transculturalexchange.org/activities/here-there-collaboration/

2008–10
Here, There and Everywhere: The Art of the Future, 100+ world sites, including Taiwan's Kuandu Museum of Fine Arts, Istanbul Metropolitan Municipality's Taksim Art Gallery, Thessaloniki's State Museum of Contemporary Art, Iran's Gallery of Mahe Mehr, Seoul's Factory, Losone's Space for Contemporary Art (Switzerland), Texas State University's CGrey Box, Atelier Moustapha Dime (as part of the 2008 Dak'Art Biennale), Tacoma's Museum of Glass, The Danish National Theatre School, the MIT Museum and Shanghai's Zendai MoMA, among others.
http://transculturalexchange.org/activities/here-there-future/

2004–8
The Tile Project, Destination: The World, 22 world sites, including New Zealand's Patak Museum, Cultural Center of the Philippines, New York City's Mercer Park, Spain's Ethnological Museum, Toronto's Wallace Emerson Park, Taipei's Kuandu Museum of Fine Arts.
www.transculturalexchange.org/tileproject

2002
The Coaster Project, Destination: The World, 100 world sites, including the Cultural Center of the Philippines, Fort Collins Museum, Colorado; Museum of Fine Arts, MA; Fuller Chicago Cultural Center, IL; PS22, NY; Artemis Art Center, Istanbul; Inner Mongolia Museum of Fine Arts, Huhhot City; and Palais de Tokyo, Paris.
www.transculturalexchange.org/coasterproject

APPENDIX

PUBLISHED ART WORK (SELECTED)

Phillips, Jayne Anne. *Lark and Termite*. London: Random House, 2009. (Drawing used as cover/front piece/inspiration.)

Lamb, Sharon. *The Trouble with Blame*. Cambridge, MA: Harvard University Press, 1996. (Painting used as cover.)

Schaeffer, Susan Fromberg. *The Madness of a Seduced Woman*. London: Penguin Books, 1991. (Painting used as cover.)

HONORS/AWARDS (SELECTED)

Boston College Office of International Programs Summer Research Grant, 2016

Berkshire Taconic Community Foundation's Artist's Resource Trust Grant, 2016

Creative Capital "On Our Radar" awardee, 2012, 2013, 2014, 2015

Fulbright Grantee, Senior Scholar Specialist, Istanbul, 2012

Fulbright 33rd Annual Conference Arts Task Force Co-Chair, Argentina, Buenos Aires, 2010
Haslla Art World, Gangneung, South Korea, Guest Artist, 2010

MA House of Representative's Certificate of Recognition, Boston, MA, 2009

The Fulbright Annual Conference, Speaker, "The Interconnected World," Beijing, China, 2008

College Board's National Arts Task Force on Arts in Education Member, 2008

Fulbright Grantee, Senior Scholar Specialist, Taiwan, 2007

Taipei Artist Village, Taiwan, International Artist-in-Residence, 2006

Harbin, China, sponsored by HIT Group, Artist-in-Residence, 2005

Quarantine Island, Turkey, Artist-in-Resident, 2004

Pilchuk School of Glass, Seattle, WA. Professional Artist-in-Residence, 2004

Massachusetts Cultural Council: Individual Artist Grants, Finalist (Painting), 2004

MIT, Cambridge, MA, Artist-in-Resident, 2002–03

Boston Cultural Council Grant, Boston, MA, 2000

BIBLIOGRAPHY (SELECTED)

2016	Abenavoli, Lorella. "*Delay* (2012) de Mary Sherman ou l'audification du regard." *ETC MEDIA* 108, *Dans les internets / Inside the Internet* (June–September 2016): p. 93. Pier, Meg. "TransCultural Exchange." *Art New England* 37, no. 1 (January/February).
2015	"The Agenda: This Week in New York." *Art in America*, July 21, 2015. Beerlink, Anna. "Forschen mit den Ohren." *Neue Zeitschrift für Musik* 5 (November): pp. 65–66.
2013	*KdMoFA Artist in Residence Program*, p. 18. Taipei: Kuandu Museum of Fine Arts, January.
2012	Holland, Christian. "Mary Sherman of TransCultural Exchange." *Art New England Online*, May 1. Accessed August 15, 2016. http://artnewengland.com/blogs/mary-sherman-of-transcultural-exchange/.

2011	"Hampden Gallery, Mary Sherman." *Fine Arts Center 2010–2011*, p. 19. Amherst: UMass Amherst. McQuaid, Cate. "Material Worlds." *The Boston Globe*, October 19.		Jaeger, Luke. "Regional Reviews." *Art New England* 25, no. 1 (January/February). Maddos, Georgina L. "Tiled Together." *Mumbai Newsline*, May 12. Pestonji, Merher. "The Tile Project." *Architecture, Time, Space & People* 4, no. 8 (August). "What's New?" *Istanbul: The Guide* (May/June).
2010	McQuaid, Cate. "Season for Living and Color." *The Boston Globe*, July 28. *Gangneung Haslla International Residency 2010*. South Korea: Haslla Open Air Museum Residency.	2003	Hopkins, Randi. "Art on Its Own." *The Boston Phoenix*, October 31. McQuaid, Cate. "Exhibition Encourages Artists to Alter One Another's Work." *The Boston Globe*, November 14.
2009	McQuaid, Cate. "Various Evidence of Enigma." *The Boston Globe*, July 22.	2002	Edgers, Geoff. "Inventiveness Spills over in *Coaster Project*." *The Boston Globe*, May 30. Knox, Robert. "Collection of Contraptions." *The Boston Globe*, September 19. Temin, Christine. "Drawing." *The Boston Globe*, January 19.
2008	*"Here Comes the Sun." Art218.com*, Shanghai. *Intrude Art* 3 and 6. Shanghai: Zendai MoMA, 2008. Catalog. Wang, Juan. "Sent Up Flying Kong Ming...." *Laodong Daily*, June 6. Yong, He. "God Bless All." *Xin-Min Evening News*, June 6.		
2006	"Seven Countries, Painters and Photographers Show." *Harbin Daily News*, p. 1, September 6. "Seven Painters and Photographers Make the Show." *Modern Evening Times*, p. A02, September 6. "Seven Painters Come to Harbin to Show Their Work." *Life Newspaper*, p. 2, September 6. Quintero, Craig. "Stage, Screen and Studio." *Radio Taiwan International*, May 17.	2001	Barber, Christina L. "Up Next." *The Daily Hampshire Gazette* (Amherst, MA), March 13. "Constructions." *The Boston Globe*, August 19. Giuliano, Charles. "Boston Gallery Hopping: Mary Sherman." *NY Arts Magazine* (January). Giuliano, Charles. "The Drawing Show." *Maverick Arts* (East Boston), December 20. Unger, Miles. "Spotlight Art: *Constructions*." *Boston Magazine*, August 2001.
2005	Interview on *The Tile Project. Formosa TV*, Taipei, May 14. McQuaid, Cate. "Dream Projects." *The Boston Globe*, p. C6, December 23. Smyth, Amanda. "Artists' Dreamscape Builds on MIT." *MIT Tech Talk*, November 16. "The Tile Project." *ARTCO Magazine*, Taiwan, June. Zhao, Ye. "*Dimensions Variable: Site Fixed*." *World Journal*, November 13.	2000	"Preview." *Art New England* 21, no. 6 (December/January). "TransCultural Exchange: Nomads Forever." *The Korean Press* (New York), August 2.
		1999	"Cultural Avenues: *nomads*." Arirang Television (Seoul), September. "*nomads*." *City Life* (Seoul), September. Stein, Stephanie. "Mastering Media as Fast..." *The South End News* (Boston), December 23. Temin, Christine. "Boston College Show..." *The Boston Globe*, July 30.
2004	Eroglu, Ozkan. "cini proseji, hedef: dunya." *Sanatsanat*, Istanbul, July. Hopkins, Randi. "Baby, It's Cold Out There." *The Boston Phoenix*, November 11. HD-TV, Ho Chi Minh City, Vietnam, December 28.		

APPENDIX

1998	"Arts and Leisure Guide Listings." *The New York Times*, July 26.
	"Divergent Paths." *The High Plains Reader* (Fargo, ND), January 29.
	"New York Reviews: no boundaries." *Artnet.com Magazine* (New York), August 3.
1997	McQuaid, Cate. "Sublimely Sinister John Lees..." *The Boston Globe*, May 15.
1995	*New American Paintings: The New England Competition*. Needham, MA: Offshore Publications. Review. RAI 3 National Italian Television, August.
1993	Alexander, M. Darsie. "The Drawing Show." *The South End News* (Boston), September 9.
1992	Doherty, Joni. "The 3rd Gloria Wilcher Memorial Exhibition." *Art New England* 13, no. 2 (February/March).
1991	Bulka, Michael. "Mary Sherman." *New Art Examiner* (Chicago), February.
	Holg, Garret. "Mary Sherman." *ARTnews* (New York), March.
	McCracken, David. "Art Review." *The Chicago Tribune*, January 4.
1989	"Kulturaktuell." Review. Austrian National Radio, October.
	"Kunsthalle Exnergasse." *Noema Art Magazine* (Vienna, Austria), September.
	"Reverse Angle." *Kunstforum*. Vienna, Austria: Kunstforum, June.
	"Vorhut ohne Ruckendeckung." *Wiener Zietung* (Vienna, Austria), October 11.